INDY CAR
C·H·A·M·P·I·O·N
A Season with Target/Chip Ganassi Racing

Ned Wicker
Photography by Cheryl Day Anderson

Motorbooks International
Publishers & Wholesalers

SO GC FP NC OB

First published in 1997 by Motorbooks International
Publishers & Wholesalers, 729 Prospect Avenue, PO Box 1,
Osceola, WI 54020-0001 USA

Motorbooks International books are also available at discounts
in bulk quantity for industrial or sales-promotional use. For
details write to Special Sales Manager at the Publisher's
address

Library of Congress Cataloging-in-Publication Data Available

ISBN 0-7603-0394-0

On the front cover: The Target car on the streets of Surfers
Paradise. Note the manhole cover behind the car. The covers
must be welded down, because Indy Cars produce enough
downforce to suck the covers right out of the hole and shoot
them 40 feet in the air.—*Cheryl Day Anderson*

On the frontispiece: Alex Zanardi at Vancouver. Alex captured
his third consecutive pole position with a 113.576 miles per
hour mark.—*Cheryl Day Anderson*

On the title page: From the top, a view into Jimmy Vasser's
"office." There is just enough room in there for the driver,
who is form-fitted into a special seat.—*Cheryl Day Anderson*

On the back cover: 1996 PPG Indy Car Champion Jimmy
Vasser, pictured here before the season in his 1995 uniform.
Teammate Alex Zanardi finished the season with three
wins.—*Cheryl Day Anderson*

Printed in Hong Kong

CONTENTS

INTRODUCTION 7

CHAPTER ONE TEAM 9

CHAPTER TWO DRIVERS 19

CHAPTER THREE EQUIPMENT 31

CHAPTER FOUR THE FEAST 37

CHAPTER FIVE 90 DAYS OF MAY 51

CHAPTER SIX THE FAMINE 59

CHAPTER SEVEN SURVIVAL 73

CHAPTER EIGHT TRIUMPH 83

STATISTICS 92

INDEX 96

Long before the 1996 PPG Indy Car World Series got underway, I firmly believed that Penske Racing was going to win the title with driver Al Unser Jr. After all, they won in 1994 and came very close to winning again in 1995. Penske is a proven commodity in this sport, so any team that wants to lay claim to the title has to push Roger Penske's guys aside. Likewise, Newman/Haas Racing with Michael Andretti is always tough, and don't forget Bobby Rahal.

I am happy to say I was completely wrong, as another team and a pair of young drivers took control of the PPG Cup Series. Target/Chip Ganassi Racing proved itself to be a powerhouse team in winning the championship, and driver Jimmy Vasser came into his own in 1996, finishing every race and establishing himself as a worthy member of Indy Car racing's elite. Newcomer Alex Zanardi came over from Italy, and played a major role in the development of the team. Along the way, he served notice through three victories and five pole positions, that he was going to be a serious contender for the title in 1997.

This book is about the anatomy of a championship, as team owner Chip Ganassi assembled all of the right pieces, put them together in the right order and earned the PPG Cup. Racing is a grind—fans only see the shimmering PPG Indy Cars on Sunday afternoons and very little of the thousands of hours it took to prepare the car for competition. Moreover, racing is the ultimate team sport, as every member of the team must do his or her job on race day to perfection, or the team doesn't win.

The Target team and its drivers became of one mind during the season, sharing the highs of four victories in the first six races by Jimmy Vasser and the crew of his #12 car, only to feel the frustrations of not being able to put a winning effort together after the U.S. 500. Alex Zanardi caught fire in the middle to late portion of the season in the #4 car, becoming the fastest car in the field in the last four races of the year. Still, there was no teammate resentment on the part of Vasser, as he watched Alex succeed so often in the latter stages of the championship season. Rather, the two drivers worked together, with engineers Morris Nunn and Julian Robertson and made the championship their mutual goal.

This book is about all of the pieces coming together. It all started back in 1994, when the Reynard chassis, Honda engines and Firestone tires began development. The successes were very few.

In 1994, if somebody had said that in two years Jimmy Vasser would become the PPG Indy Car World Series champion, using Firestone tires and a Honda engine, I would have thought them crazy. Back then, the Honda engine was in development and Rahal-Hogan Racing couldn't finish a race with it because of severe reliability problems. What's worse, the Honda didn't make any power in its first year, so it was both slow and unreliable.

What happened between 1994, and the victory circle celebration by Target/Chip Ganassi Racing after Jimmy Vasser clinched the 1996 title?

Somehow, in 1996, Target/Chip Ganassi Racing was not the "middle of the road" team which had done little to capture anyone's imagination in the early 1990s, but had emerged into a powerhouse team, with all of the right elements for success in the PPG Cup Series.

Hopefully, when you have finished this book, you will have a better idea why Jimmy Vasser won the 1996 title and everything it takes to be a champion in the PPG Cup.

CHAPTER ONE

THE TEAM

Long before a team can begin to think about winning races and placing the PPG Cup in its trophy case, it has to assemble all of the right pieces to the Indy Car puzzle, from having the right driver behind the wheel to having the right equipment configuration on the race track. Indy Car racing is a highly competitive industry and the differences between winning and losing in this business are sometimes as narrow as having the right set of tires put on the car during the last pit stop of the last race.

Like other Indy Car teams, Target/Chip Ganassi Racing begins with its owner, Chip Ganassi. Indy Car team owners are very similar to owners of other sports franchises, because they are responsible for the financial end of the business. Baseball clubs need the best players and the necessary equipment to win, and the same is true for an Indy Car team. Ganassi, like many other team owners in the PPG Cup, wears many hats in addition to his main role as head of the Target/Chip Ganassi Racing organization. He is the executive vice president of the FRG group,

which is a Pittsburgh-based holding company with interests in telecommunications, manufacturing and computer business. Ganassi also owns a small piece of the Pittsburgh Pirates National League Baseball Club.

Although he had been a full-time Indy Car driver in the early 1980s, Ganassi was first a college graduate, earning a degree in finance from Duquense University in 1982, the same year he moved up to Indy Cars as a driver.

Ganassi came to the PPG Cup in 1982, driving for Jack Rhoades. His best performance of the year was an eleventh place finish at the Cleveland Grand Prix, but he was able to qualify for the Indianapolis 500 in his rookie season and finished fifteenth. All told, he ran five races that year, but was hardly a threat to challenge other rookies in the series that year.

The following year, Ganassi got a good break by signing with the powerful Patrick Racing team, whose driver, Gordon Johncock, was one of the top drivers in the series. This time, Chip

As Jimmy Vasser sped by after taking the checkered flag at Surfers Paradise in Queensland, Australia, the crew jumped over the wall and celebrated the victory. It was a dominating win for Vasser, who won the pole position and led most of the race.

The crew of the #12 car: (left to right) Geoff Carter, Grant Weaver (crew chief), Scott Harner, Jim Perry, Al Modey, Tim Keene, Jim Hayhoe (behind), Jimmy Vasser (in car), Jackie Cobb, Leonard Gauci, Tom Vasi, Jeff Stafford and Devan Price (not shown, Gary Neal).

competed in 10 of the 13 races, and showed his talent, finishing third at both Laguna Seca Raceway and at the street course in the parking lot of Caesar's Palace in Las Vegas. His eighth place finish at Indianapolis was also major, and his peers voted him "Most Improved Driver."

Chip's racing career in Indy Cars was rather short-lived, as a horrifying crash at the Michigan International Speedway in 1984 nearly killed him. He and Al Unser Jr. got tangled together coming off the second turn at the high-banked, two-mile oval, then slid across the infield grass and flipped several times before crashing into the inside retaining barrier.

Prior to the crash at Michigan that year, Ganassi started seven races and had collected his career best finish, a second at Cleveland. After the

accident, Chip spent the rest of the year recuperating, but came back to Indy Car racing the following year, running the Indianapolis 500 for A.J. Foyt, and the Michigan 500 for the Machinists Union team. He started the first two races of the 1986 season for the Machinists Union team, but then stepped out of the car. He did, however, run in four International Motor Sports Association (IMSA) events later that year.

The love of Indy Car racing was a powerful force, and in 1988, Chip returned to the Patrick Racing team, not as a driver, but as an owner, buying into the Patrick Racing team. It was then that Chip established key relationships that would lead to the formation of his own team in two years.

The crew of the #4 car: (left to right) Rob Hill (crew chief), Floyd Ganassi, Dan Lewis, Wayne Westplate, Steve Gough, Simon Hodgson, Brad Filbey, Ricky Davis, Brian Whittemore, John Wayne Gape, Dan Hammond, Doug Forker.

Chip's first experience as a team owner was far better than most, as the Patrick Racing operation, using the Penske PC18 chassis and the Chevrolet Indy V-8 engine, was the dominant force in the series. Owner U.E. "Pat" Patrick had been through it all before, winning races and championships. It was the perfect situation for a young car owner to be in to observe and learn.

Driver Emerson Fittipaldi won the Indianapolis 500 and went on to collect wins at Detroit, Portland, Cleveland and Nazareth. Fittipaldi clinched the PPG Indy Car World Series title at Nazareth. Interestingly, in the post race press conference, Chip represented ownership, not the venerable Patrick. This was Patrick's team and Chip was in the background most of

the season and did not receive credit for his role in the title chase.

With no more mountains to climb, Patrick wanted a change, so he opted to take over the Indy Car engine development program for Alfa Romeo. Rather than moving the Alfa Romeo operation into his shop near 38th Street and I-65, Patrick sold his shop and his team franchise to Chip and kept the Alfa program in its existing home on Gasoline Alley. The parting of the ways between Chip and Patrick also meant some team members had to make a choice between going to the development operation, or staying at the same building, under new management.

Veteran team manager Jim McGee, who had been with Patrick for years, chose to go with

Joe Montana and Chip Ganassi have become fast friends since Joe came to the team in 1995. Joe is always asking questions and has an insatiable appetite for racing information.

Patrick. That left Ganassi without a team manager, but the position was quickly filled by Tom Anderson, who was Fittipaldi's crew chief during the championship season. Anderson has been involved in the PPG Indy Car World Series since 1980, when he was a crew member on Jim Hall's PPG Cup and Indy 500 championship team. It

Jim Hayhoe (left) has played a major role in advancing Jimmy Vasser's career over the years. Hayhoe fielded his own team for a couple of years, with marginal success. He made the deal with Chip Ganassi (right) to bring Vasser to the team in 1995.

was Anderson's job to assemble the crew and run the operation.

The first Target-sponsored Ganassi Racing car came on the PPG Cup scene in 1990, as Chip hired American driver Eddie Cheever, a veteran of Formula One, to pilot his car. The paint scheme was interesting, as from the side, it looked like a white car with wavy red stripes, but from the top, it was clearly the familiar Target logo. Cheever had a good rookie season in the series, winning both the Indianapolis 500 and CART "Rookie of the Year" honors. He finished ninth in the point standings in 1990, then ninth again in 1992.

In 1992, Cheever and the team were not making significant progress, and for the most part, Cheever was not considered to be a factor in the hunt for the championship. Shortly before the Texaco/Havoline 200 at Road America, Chip informed Cheever that a change was coming and that he would not be a part of the team's future. The team had hired 1990 Indy 500 winner Arie Luyendyk to drive part time, and it was evident that Luyendyk was getting better results. Ganassi also fielded a second car at selected events for Robby Gordon, who was getting a push into Indy Car racing from Ford, but the arrangement was only temporary.

Arie Luyendyk was the team's main driver in 1993, and rewarded his boss with a pole position at the Indianapolis 500, but it was clearly evident that Ganassi would have to raise the level of play for his teams. Chip announced his intentions of bringing the Reynard chassis into Indy car racing at the 1993 Budweiser/G.I. Joe's 200. He introduced Adrian Reynard to the media, as well as Bruce Ashmore, a designer from Lola, who moved over to the newly created Reynard North America, to serve as technical director. Although Ganassi's Lola chassis was very good, he was looking for something that could beat the Lola and give his team an edge.

Carl Haas, the north American distributor for Lola at the time, clearly had an advantage because of all the development time the team had spent on behalf of Lola. However, at the time,

Chip Ganassi (left) is a minority owner of the Pittsburgh Pirates National League Baseball Club, while Joe Montana became a legend in the National Football League, playing for the San Francisco 49'ers and the Kansas City Chiefs. Their outside sports preferences produced this comical photo opportunity early in the season.

there was a great deal of grumbling among the rank and file of Lola teams, as owners felt Haas was not sharing enough information, and that the technical data that was passed along to the other teams was being delayed. The Reynard operation in the PPG Cup would be different, as there would be a much closer relationship between the manufacturer and the customer. The competitive upside was that if one Reynard team found something that would improve the car, in regards to the design of the car, Reynard would implement the changes. Of course, individual tricks of the trade and setups were proprietary.

As the 1993 season was coming to a close, Ganassi made another strong move in signing 1991 PPG Cup champion Michael Andretti, who had been competing in Formula One during the 1993 season, but by September, had already parted company with his F1 team, McLaren. Andretti was officially introduced as the team's driver for 1994 in a press conference during the race weekend at Nazareth, Michael's hometown. However, when Andretti moved in, there was no longer room for Luyendyk, who was not renewed for the following season.

The Reynard launch was highly successful, as Michael Andretti, driving for Ganassi, won the very first race for the Reynard chassis. The race was stopped twice by rain, and by the time Michael flashed by the starter's stand and took the checkered flag, the street lights at Surfers Paradise were

Tom Anderson (left) runs the racing operation for Chip Ganassi (right) and called the strategy during the races for driver Jimmy Vasser. Ganassi was on the radio with Alex Zanardi.

During the 1995 and 1996 seasons, managing director Tom Anderson developed a strong professional relationship with his driver, Jimmy Vasser. The two are not close off the track, but have a strong racing bond between them during business hours.

already on, and the sun had already set over the Queensland, Australia horizon. The Michael Andretti/Ganassi combination produced another victory at the Molson Indy Toronto, but Michael already had his heart set on returning to New-man/Haas Racing, his home from 1989 to 1992. Ganassi had a second car, driven by Mauricio Gugelmin, but it was a completely separate operation, as Andretti preferred a one-car team.

When Michael returned to Newman/Haas, and Gugelmin was signed by the new PacWest Racing team, Ganassi had to start building again. He chose Bryan Herta, the 1993 PPG-Firestone Indy Lights champion, and a younger driver who was widely regarded as a major up and coming talent. Herta had driven a few races in 1994, mostly for A.J. Foyt, but a serious crash in Toronto ended his season and put a large question mark on his fitness for the following year. But Herta's marks were very high and Ganassi was looking to build his team around a young driver.

Shortly after the 1995 PPG Indy Car World Series got underway, Target/Chip Ganassi Racing picked up another key member of the championship equation. In April, just one week after he announced his retirement from the National Football League, quarterback Joe Montana traded his red Kansas City Chiefs jersey for the red Target colors in the PPG Cup. Montana met fellow Pittsburgh native Chip Ganassi at a celebrity race in Long Beach in early 1995. The subsequent partnership was started, fulfilling a long-time dream of Montana's to become a part of the racing scene.

Montana is a team partner, meaning his involvement is financial, but his understanding of the athlete's mind and his ability to coach players in times of extreme pressure have proven to be an invaluable part of the team's success over the last two years.

"Being a part of this team has really helped my transition from football," said Montana at a luncheon after the 1996 season. However, unlike fellow Indy Car team owner and NFL Hall of Fame running back Walter Payton, Montana does not see himself as a driver. Payton ran Sports 2000 cars, then competed on the Sports Car Club of America's TransAm Series before becoming a

A driver's gestures tell all about what the car is doing in the corners, and Alex Zanardi is rather animated in communicating the situation to engineer Morris Nunn.

team owner. Ironically, had Montana been a race car driver, at his age, although long past his prime as an NFL quarterback, he would be in the height of his racing career.

"Yes, but I would have had to start 20 years ago," he said, quickly adding that he is content to watch Jimmy Vasser and Alex Zanardi and has no urge to drive himself.

Montana has given the team a higher degree of visibility through his work on team marketing programs, business promotions and sponsor relations.

The key mechanics of the group were assembled. In 1995, Mike Hull was the chief mechanic for Bryan Herta, but was promoted to team manager prior to the start of the 1996 season. Prior to his tenure with Target/Chip Ganassi Racing, Hull worked with PPG Cup teams Arciero Racing, Patrick Racing, Hayhoe Racing and Rahal-Hogan Racing. Hull also has experience in Super Vee racing and the PPG-Firestone Indy Lights.

Indy Car racing is an engineer-driven series, which means that the race engineers who setup the cars are probably the most important technical per-

One of the driving forces behind Target/Chip Ganassi is Chip's father, Floyd (left). A highly successful businessman and entrepreneur, a lot of Floyd is in Chip, who knows there's no better consultant for his team than his father.

sonnel in the sport. Perhaps no other engineer in Indy Car racing is as widely known and respected as Morris Nunn. Nunn, age 58, has been involved in the PPG cup since 1984, when he came over from the Ensign Formula One team to direct the Bignotti-Cotter racing engineering team. In 1989, he and driver Emerson Fittipaldi won the PPG Cup and the Indy 500 together, while with Patrick Racing. In 1996, Nunn was the engineer for Alex Zanardi's #4 Target car, but as chief engineer, was responsible for both cars.

Englishman Julian Robertson, age 33, was the engineer on Jimmy Vasser's #12 car, and the two combined for four podium finishes and four front-row qualifying berths in 1995. The stage was set for bigger things in 1996. With the addition of the Honda, and the new Firestone tires, they picked up where they left off in 1995. Robertson's setups and Vasser's heavy foot contributed to four victories and four poles on the way to the 1996 PPG Cup title.

Julian has been with Target/Chip Ganassi Racing since mid-1993, after a brief stint with Dick Simon Racing. He engineered the first victory for the Reynard chassis in 1994, with Michael Andretti at the wheel. In 1995, his driver won the "Most Improved Driver" award.

Grant Weaver, age 39, became Jimmy Vasser's chief mechanic in 1995 and the combination clicked

in 1996, winning four races and the PPG Cup. Weaver has been involved in major racing series since 1981, and also spent some time in sports car racing.

Australian Rob Hill, age 35, came to Target/Chip Ganassi Racing from the Rahal-Hogan Racing team after the 1995 season. He also had a stint with Patrick Racing in the PPG Cup, but came to Indy Car racing from Formula Two. Rob had a scare before the Toronto race, when he suddenly went into cardiac arrest from a complication of Lyme's Disease. He was fitted with a pacemaker and recovered fully.

When Jimmy Vasser came to the team, he brought Jim Hayhoe, or vice versa. Hayhoe is not known to racing fans, nor is he a particularly high profile member of the team, but his impact on Target/Chip Ganassi Racing is undeniable.

Hayhoe's relationship with Vasser began the night before the 1991 Toyota Grand Prix of Long Beach when, at the request of Rick Galles, Hayhoe entertained Galles' son, Jamie and a couple of his friends, Stewart Crow and Jimmy, aboard Hayhoe's boat. Vasser, then a Toyota Atlantic driver, met Hayhoe for the first time. Hayhoe, who had fielded Indy Cars in the 1960s, became interested in Jimmy's driving career. Once Hayhoe saw Vasser's talent, he was hooked.

Engineer Julian Robertson, Jimmy Vasser and Tom Anderson discuss how to get more speed out of the Target car after a practice session. Julian has an idea, which Tom seems to agree with, but Jimmy isn't so sure.

Tom Anderson (left) and the crew congratulated each other after Jimmy Vasser's victory in Australia. The big fellow on the right is Bill Luchow, a CART official, who works the pit lane during the races to make sure the pit stops are done correctly.

Vasser drove for Hayhoe in the PPG Cup between 1992-1994, but it was obvious to Hayhoe that the only way Vasser would flourish in the series would be to hook up with a first-rate team, with the proper sponsorship. Although Hayhoe had a small measure of sponsorship for Jimmy, it was not enough to be competitive in the Indy Car world, so he made the deal with Chip Ganassi.

Hayhoe was instrumental in putting together the arrangements for the team's use of the Honda engines in 1996, and is almost Ganassi's right arm on the business end of the operation.

Ganassi assembled a strong organization, from Tom Anderson down to the apprentice mechanics who are not a part of the traveling team. Over the first six years of the team's existence, all of the human elements for a championship were assembled. Now it was time for Ganassi to see to it that his mechanical equipment was capable of beating the best teams in the world.

The prize for winning the inaugural U.S. 500 on Memorial Day weekend was $1 million. Chip Ganassi, Jimmy Vasser and the crew of the #12 car collected their prize. Alex Zanardi was leading the race handily, but had engine failure. However, all winning shares are distributed evenly between the two cars.

"I've got the best team in the business."
Chip Ganassi Owner
Target/Chip Ganassi Racing

CHAPTER TWO

THE DRIVERS

When Jimmy Vasser joined Target/Chip Ganassi Racing in 1995, it was long after the team had chosen second-year driver Bryan Herta as its main talent. But Vasser's consistency in 1995, and the lack of results by Herta's side of the team, prompted Chip Ganassi to look to Vasser to carry the load in 1996.

Jimmy's physical characteristics are typical of an Indy Car driver, as he is 5 feet 9 inches tall and weighs 155 pounds. He has the look of the all-American boy next door, with medium length brown hair. He isn't a fancy guy, whose taste in clothes leans more towards t-shirts and jeans, than designer threads. He is similar to many of the younger drivers in the series, coming up through Formula Fords and go karts before reaching a stepping stone series to the PPG Cup—in Vasser's case, the Toyota Atlantic Championship.

Vasser had been driving since he was six years old. In 1974, when he was eight, Vasser won the national quarter midget championship, and repeated that effort in 1975. He won a third quarter midget championship in 1978, before going through the Jim Russell school and moving up to Formula Fords. In 1984, he was competing in the Formula Ford Pro Championship and won rookie of the year honors and the national title. He won the SCCA's national Formula Ford title again in 1986, then moved on to the SCCA's Formula Atlantic series where he finished second in the point standings in 1987. Vasser drover Formula Fords and Pro Sports 2000 in the United States and Canada the next couple of years before moving up to the Toyota Atlantic Championship Series in 1990. The year he met Jim Hayhoe, he scored six victories and eight poles, and was awarded the Gilles Villeneuve trophy. While many would argue that most drivers aren't ready to jump to Indy Cars after two seasons of the Toyota Atlantics, clearly Vasser was the exception to the rule.

Because of that, Hayhoe decided to form his own Indy Car team and run his newfound driver, but that would prove to be more of a lesson in frustration than a push towards bigger and brighter days at the major league level.

Chip Ganassi and his drivers, Alex Zanardi (left) and Jimmy Vasser (right) posed during the front row photo shoot the day before the Marlboro 500.

From the very beginning of their relationship, drivers Jimmy Vasser (left) and Alex Zanardi (right) shared everything about their individual cars to make the team stronger. Listening in is Michael Knight, widely regarded as the sport's finest public relations professional.

Vasser showed sparks of being an exceptional talent, but Hayhoe's operation never had the kind of sponsorship that would allow Jimmy to run a full season, do the testing and development work, and be competitive with the biggest and best of the PPG Cup. At Indianapolis, he broke his leg during a crash and missed three of the next four races. He ran 12 races in 1993, then all 16 races in 1994 and scored a fourth place finish at Australia and Indianapolis.

Still Hayhoe kept plugging away, hoping something would land for his driver, either a major sponsorship package or a stronger team. During those three seasons with Hayhoe Racing, arrangements were made with Dick Simon Racing to help with the maintenance and preparation of the car.

Jimmy Vasser and the Target-Reynard. Note all of the associate sponsors on the car. Racing at the top requires the necessary funding and teams develop mutually beneficial relationships with sponsors.

Vasser did turn some heads in 1993 by actually leading the point standings early in the season, but the team never had the kind of financial footing that would allow it to move up to the next level of competitiveness.

After the 1994 season, Hayhoe made the deal with Chip Ganassi. In addition to Vasser's driving abilities, the team got a significant bonus in Hayhoe, whose business expertise would produce major impact changes for the operation. Hayhoe would become a central figure in the success ahead.

Going into 1996, two elements were in place from the 1995 season—driver Jimmy Vasser and the Reynard chassis. Bryan Herta struggled in 1995 and his contract was not renewed. The team was looking for a second driver and tested several, with Alex Zanardi and Jeff Krosnoff scoring high marks in a post-season test at Homestead, Florida. Zanardi had come highly recommended from Reynard, who had worked with the Italian driver in Formula 3000.

The relationship between Zanardi and Ganassi flourished, almost from the very beginning, as their Italian temperaments seemed to match. It was Ganassi who described Zanardi as the most "non-Italian, Italian" he had ever worked with, noting that Zanardi was not a hot-head under fire and had a much more even temperament than many of his countrymen. He is a half-inch taller than Jimmy, and two pounds heavier, but very much in the same mold. Alex's deep-set, dark eyes and dark brown hair give him a typical Italian look. He is friendly and has an engaging smile. His slight lisp is not at all a speech impediment as much as it is a charming accent to his personality. While some competitors

From the very first race of the season, Jimmy Vasser knew he had a good combination with the Reynard chassis, Honda engine and Firestone tires.

Alex Zanardi came to Indy Car racing via Formula 3000, where he had developed a solid relationship with Reynard.

Alex Zanardi gets some instructions from Morris Nunn in preparation for qualifying for the U.S. 500. Before 1996, Alex had never driven ovals or been on a superspeedway, like the high-banked Michigan International Speedway.

in Formula One are regarded as unapproachable, Zanardi fit right into the Indy Car culture.

Keeping the "Italian" element in mind, and considering Zanardi's background in racing, the team decided to give him the ride, not knowing that the addition of Zanardi would soon prove to be one of the best moves Ganassi had ever made.

Alex had impeccable credentials. Like many other drivers, Zanardi got started in karting, and in his first year, 1980, won some national events in Italy. By 1984, he was on the international scene, winning races in Hong Kong, France and Germany. The next year he won titles in Italy, Europe and Australia. He advanced through the go kart ranks, to the top of the European ladder. Then in 1988, he jumped to Italian Formula Three. By 1990, he

was consistently winning F3 races all over Europe, prompting a move up to the FIA Formula 3000 in 1991, where Alex began his relationship with Reynard. He qualified on the front row in nine of the ten races in the series, won twice and finished second in four other races. Three mechanical failures that year cost him the title, which went to another future Formula One and PPG Cup driver, Christian Fittipaldi. Formula One team owner Eddie Jordan hired Zanardi for the final three races of the season, and Alex finished ninth in his first race.

In 1992, Alex became the test driver for Benetton, and drove in a replacement role for the injured Fittipaldi in three events for Minardi. The next year, he moved to Lotus, and scored his first point in Formula One competition with a sixth

The debriefing sessions after practice and qualifying are vital to the success of the team, and drivers Jimmy Vasser (right) and Alex Zanardi shared everything about their cars. Chip Ganassi (left) insisted that his drivers and engineers (that's Mo Nunn standing in the background) be a complete team with no secrets and no hidden agendas.

place finish in Brazil. Then, a major crash in Belgium put him on the sidelines. He recovered from the injuries and went back to Lotus as the test driver in 1994. Four races into the season, he had the ride, subbing once again for an injured driver, this time Pedro Lamy. However, Lotus was in financial turmoil and the team went into receivership, closing its doors and putting Alex out on the street. He ran in the British Racing Production championship in 1995, in the GT2 class. His personal relationships with the Reynard people served him well, as Reynard directed him to Target/Chip Ganassi Racing.

Ganassi had two drivers, similar in their physical makeup, but with different skill sets. Vasser brought years of oval racing experience to the team, while Zanardi was expert on road courses. Vasser is a quick driver, but Zanardi probably has a more aggressive streak in him, as would come out in the final race of the season. It would be the melding of their skills that would make the Vasser/Zanardi combination the most formidable in the PPG Cup for 1996.

One of the factors that impressed the team when they first tested Alex was his ability to read and understand the race car, and his ability to work with the car and improve the setup. He is more intense than Vasser in the sense that one can often spot Alex in the transporter debriefing with Morris Nunn long after other drivers have gone back to the hotel. He is one of those drivers who has to know

Driver Alex Zanardi developed an exceptional professional relationship with engineer Morris Nunn. Zanardi was the runaway selection for the 1996 Friends of Jim Trueman "Rookie of the Year" Award.

everything about the car and is always completely involved in every technical aspect of the operation.

For Zanardi, family played an important role in his becoming a race car driver. Following the death of his sister, Christina, who was killed in an automobile accident in 1979, the Zanardi family became closer. Alex developed an interest in racing, and his parents bought him a go kart and took an interest in his racing activities.

"Christina's death affected not only me, but my father and mother as well," said Zanardi. "You can probably imagine how bad it was. But karting was something that held the attention of the family all the time. At every single lunch and dinner, we were talking about the go-kart. My mother was working just to make some money to buy the go-kart. That's why my career started. If my father would have known what my future would be, I don't know if he would have made a different choice."

Jimmy Vasser battled Al Unser Jr. at the U.S. 500. Jimmy won that day, but Unser, a two-time PPG Cup champion, took him down to the wire in the season point race.

Jimmy Vasser was always around the car between sessions. Note the rain tires he's sitting on during an obviously sunny day. Those are used when rolling the car back and forth from the pits.

Vasser's career was also a family affair. His father, Jim Sr., was a drag racer and Jimmy used to go to the races and cheer him on. Naturally, it was an easy decision for Jim Sr. to put his six-year-old son in that quarter midget. Through the years, the two worked together in all forms of racing, but there was not a lot of family money to invest in the racing program, so moving up the ladder was difficult. However, Jimmy's values were deep-rooted, and because so much of the success he had in racing during the early days had to do with his own knowledge and ability, Vasser became a strong technical racer.

Likewise, Vasser is tenacious as a competitor, but is not as likely to execute a high-risk maneuver unless he is satisfied that the results will be positive. Because he began racing so early in life, Jimmy's racing skills are second nature. He has gone well beyond the mere ability to drive and handle an Indy Car at the highest level of competition. Vasser is a racer, with a competitive heart equal to that of any other sporting champion. For a car owner, one of Jimmy's most endearing qualities is his consistency, as demonstrated in 1996. He scored in all but one race, and finished every race. Other than the crash before the start of the U.S. 500, Vasser didn't put a scratch on the car and still won the championship. If a driver runs at or near the front, finishes most of the races and doesn't crash, chances are he'll be in the thick of any point chase.

Jimmy is never too happy when he wins, and never too down when he loses. His lack of emotion is sometimes mistaken for nonchalance, such as his off the cuff comment after winning the U.S. 500, "Who needs milk?" which was mistaken for arrogance and taken as a swipe against the Indy 500. Vasser is a blue collar guy, who along with his father, built a racing career from the ground up and made it to the top without the assistance of big money. He is a refreshing change of pace, as he made the big time on talent alone.

Alex Zanardi was always too serious and never allowed himself to have fun during the year.

Jimmy Vasser was excited to get that first victory and shared the moment with Chip Ganassi (left) and Joe Montana (right). Gil de Ferran (far right) finished second and Robby Gordon (far left) was third.

Jimmy Vasser #12
Birthdate: November 20, 1963
Height: 5'9"
Weight: 155lb.
Residence: San Francisco and Puyallup, Washington (Jimmy moved to Las Vegas in late 1996)
Marital Status: Single
Children: None
Family: Parents, Jim Vasser and Roxanne Collins; Sisters, Candice and Viki; Brother, Pat.
Hobbies: Golf, skiing, classic car restoration
Personal Automobiles: Acura and 1957 Thunderbird

Alex Zanardi #4
Birthdate: October 23, 1966
Height: 5' 9 1/2"
Weight: 157lb.
Marital Status: Married, November 1996
Children: None
Hobbies: Mountain biking, fishing, model aircraft
Personal Automobiles: BMW 525, BMW 318, Cagiva E-900 Elefant

CHAPTER THREE

THE EQUIPMENT

For the Target/Chip Ganassi Racing team, the most important moves for the 1996 season were made in the fall of 1995. Throughout the 1995 PPG Indy Car World Series season, Ganassi's drivers suffered through a myriad of mechanical maladies, starting with a mysterious glitch in the manufacturing of the gearboxes in the Reynard chassis. However, the most frustrating experience of that year was the failure of the Ford Cosworth XD engines to live up to expectations. The XB Series I and II engines, used from 1992-1994, might not have been much of a horsepower rival to the Mercedes-Benz, but at least they held together. The XD, which made its debut in 1995, had serious reliability questions all year long. In fact, Ganassi's season ended at Laguna Seca with an electrical failure, but by then owner Chip Ganassi was well on his way to deciding that Ford was not in his plans for 1996.

It became apparent during the 1995 season that the chassis were very closely matched, as Reynard, Lola and the Penske all won races. Engine reliability was paramount for the Ganassi team, but Chip was reluctant to switch engine manufacturers because his team had been the development team for Ford-Cosworth.

Meanwhile, Jim Hayhoe had been interested in the Honda program since the first year Honda came into the sport in 1994. Hayhoe liked the organization and saw the development path, even though Rahal/Hogan and Comptech Racing, who had use of the Honda in 1994, experienced every kind of mechanical problem and, in the case of Rahal/Hogan, had a dismal season. Comptech was a development team, which got to run a few, selected races, so little was expected of them. Jim Hayhoe, while still running his own car in 1994, was looking to put any kind of a deal together that would give his team an edge. He was in a position to make the deal to use the Honda, but with a lack of sponsorship and having to take more of a personal investment angle in the team, Hayhoe decided to back off. When he and Vasser moved to Ganassi in 1995, Hayhoe immediately began working on the Honda engine program, but he would have to sell the idea to Ganassi.

Looking down at Jimmy Vasser's Target Reynard-Honda from the rooftops of Surfers Paradise. Jimmy's car and Alex Zanardi's cars were so similar, that the team later painted Jimmy's roll hoop yellow to tell them apart.

The team used 1996 Honda Indy V-8 engines during the 1996 season. This was a switch from the Ford Cosworth XD engines used in the 1995 season. The XD had had reliability problems all year. When the team ended the 1995 season at Laguna Seca with an electrical failure, Ganassi was well on his way to deciding Ford was not in the picture for 1996.

Gary Neal, Jim Perry, and Devin Price work on Jimmy Vasser's car between sessions at Vancouver. Jimmy had a frustrating weekend, finishing seventh.

The Target Reynard chassis, Honda Indy V-8 engine and Firestone tires proved to be the winning combination for the Target/Chip Ganassi team. The cars weigh 1,550 pounds and have a top speed of approximately 240 miles per hour. The cars run on methanol fuel.

In 1995, the Honda was being used by the Tasman Motorsports Group and Brix-Comptech Racing. Tasman had the most success, with a front row appearance at the Indianapolis 500, and a victory at New Hampshire. Comptech got on the map when Parker Johnstone won the pole at the Marlboro 500, and almost overnight, became a racing celebrity. Clearly, Honda was making major gains in 1995, and Hayhoe wanted Ganassi to take a look for the 1996 season. By the fall of 1995, the Indy Car community was buzzing about the enormous horsepower that the Honda engine was beginning to develop, a point that did not go unnoticed by the other manufacturers in the series. Hayhoe urged Ganassi to put the program together, but Ganassi was vacillating. However, by the Laguna Seca race, after a year of engine failures, Ganassi shook hands with the Honda people.

Chip Ganassi had his drivers, the Honda engine and the Reynard chassis in place for the 1996 season. But there was one more move that would prove to be significant—a switch from Goodyear tires to Firestone tires. Ganassi had a long-standing relationship with Goodyear, so making any change in that area would require significant substantiation.

"We felt that no matter what we did, we would be at best forth or fifth on the food chain with Goodyear and we felt that wasn't good enough," said Tom Anderson, in describing all of the options the team had on the table at the time. "We wanted to be more involved with tire development with our chassis and we knew we wouldn't be on the top of Goodyear's list."

From the management and engineering standpoint, the tire change was an easy one, but politically, it was more difficult for Ganassi. But the fact remained that Firestone had turned heads in 1995. Scott Pruett, driving for Patrick Racing, the Firestone development team, captured the first victory for Firestone, who returned to the sport of Indy Car racing after a 21-year hiatus. Pruett also spent a good portion of the season in the PPG Cup point lead. Pruett's win in the Marlboro 500 demonstrated Firestone's performance advantage over Goodyear in the latter stages of race segments. Over the first 10 laps after a pit stop, the tires were virtually the same, but the Firestone-clad cars picked up a competitive advantage the longer the cars were on the track. In the final 10 laps before a pit stop, or the end of the race, Firestone drivers enjoyed higher performance than their Goodyear counterparts.

Actually, Firestone's impressive high-speed runs and reliability were clearly evident at the 1995 Indianapolis 500, as Tasman Motorsports Group driver Scott Goodyear was clearly the fastest and most dominant car in the race as the event wore down to the final laps. Of course, much of Goodyear's speed at Indy was due to the performance of the Honda engine. Goodyear, however, committed a fatal error by passing the pace car on a restart late in the race, and was consequently black-flagged by the United States Auto Club for the infraction. Jacques Villeneuve, who was running second, was then declared the winner of the race.

The Ganassi people watched the Firestone progress with extreme interest and felt that they were possibly a stronger team than either Patrick or Tasman, and did not have any reservation about making the switch to Firestone. Anderson knew his team would be competitive and up to the task of winning a few races. As it turned out, they won it all.

Once the equipment package was put in place, the team awaited the delivery of the 1996 Reynard-Honda, but immediately retro-fitted a 1995 car to accommodate the Honda engine and went testing in October and November. The concerns about the extra weight of the Honda engine over the Ford-Cosworth XD was quickly relieved, as it was determined that any additional weight in the engine could be taken off the car in other places, to avoid any competitive disadvantage by being over weight. Vasser knew he had a shot at being competitive, knowing the capabilities of the package the team had assembled.

"I thought we had a good chance to be in the hunt," said Vasser. "Chip made some bold moves during the off-season to get Honda engines and Firestone tires. I felt putting those elements together with the Target Reynard chassis would give us a good package of chassis, engine and tires. In fact, Parker Johnstone was the only other driver with that package. I knew if it came together, we'd have an advantage because there weren't a lot of other people out there with the same thing we had. The other thing I felt good about was I was working

Michihiro Asaka (left), the executive vice president of Honda visits with driver Alex Zanardi.

Success in racing is often based on relationships. Team owner Chip Ganassi (left) developed a strong rapport with the Firestone people, especially Al Speyer, the manager of racing for Bridgestone/Firestone.

The power behind the Target team was Honda. Robert Clarke of Honda Performance Development talked with Jim Hayhoe, who was instrumental in bringing the Honda deal to the team, and driver Alex Zanardi.

with the same group of people for the second year in-a-row and I hadn't had that advantage before. Tom Anderson, Julian Robertson and Grant Weaver and I had built a relationship during 1995 and we were comfortable working together."

Target/Chip Ganassi Racing had all of its elements in place, but the team was very late getting out on the race track with the new configuration, although an extensive amount of testing with the Honda engine had taken place in the fall of 1995. The testing program as a whole was not as aggressive as that of some other PPG Cup teams, and certainly not what managing director Tom Anderson thought was an acceptable amount. The team was a little behind because only one 1996 car was available early in the new year for Jimmy Vasser, and newcomer Alex Zanardi did most of his testing in the 1995 car. The reason for this was because the team was very late in changing engine manufacturers, and thus, the orders for the new cars had to be delayed. Reynard manufactures each car to fit a specific engine, the Honda, Mercedes-Benz, or the Ford-Cosworth. The mounting of each engine is unique, so it is not simply a matter of fitting one engine or another on the car. Ganassi, by waiting to make his decision, was in the back of the line, so to speak, and had to wait for the delivery of all the orders preceding his. The team took delivery on three chassis in late February, the last of which was not delivered until the week before the opening race of the season at the Homestead Motorsports Complex.

The late delivery of the cars put an additional load on the Target team, but as it turned out, other teams had delivery problems as well, so the experience of the Ganassi team was not unlike that of some others. Zanardi saw his first 1996 car shortly before the Homestead race, and the team wanted some more preparation time. But the season was upon them and it was time to do it for real.

The team switched from Goodyear to Firestone tires for 1996. Firestone tires turned heads in 1995, posting a first victory since their 21-year hiatus from the sport of Indy Car racing. It was found that cars with Firestone tires picked up a competitive advantage the longer the cars were on the track. In the final 10 laps before a pit stop, or the end of the race, Firestone drivers seemed to enjoy higher performance than their Goodyear counterparts.

There were also a couple of late administrative changes, which were more formality than anything else. Prior to the start of the 1996 season, Anderson was elevated to the position of managing director, as Mike Hull, who was the crew chief for Bryan Herta, was promoted to team manager. Rob Hill then took over as the chief mechanic for Zanardi's #4 car, joining Grant Weaver, who was crew chief on Jimmy's #12.

It's one thing to have all of the right elements in place, but it's quite another to go out and run against many of the finest racing teams in the world. The first event of the season would be a brand new event at the newly-completed Metro-Dade Homestead Motorsports Complex. Out of the destruction of Hurricane Andrew came economic revitalization with this new facility, which had been built by Ralph Sanchez, who rallied local, county and state government together to make the project work.

Ready or not, it was showtime.

> "I thought we had a good chance to be in the hunt. Chip made some bold moves during the off-season to get Honda engines and Firestone tires. I felt putting those elements together with the Target Reynard chassis would give us a good package of chassis, engine and tires."
> Jimmy Vasser
> Driver #12

THE FEAST

Every race in the PPG Indy Car World Series counts the same, meaning that in terms of the season championship, no one race is worth more than another. In 1996, there were 16 races comprising the PPG Cup, so teams only had 16 opportunities to score points and earn their way to the title. While every team wants to win, the object is to score and Target/Chip Ganassi Racing and driver Jimmy Vasser did just that in the first third of the season. In fact, no driver since Mario Andretti in 1984 did any better.

Race 1
March 3
Marlboro Grand Prix of Miami
Metro Dade Homestead Motorsports Complex
Homestead, Florida
1.5-mile Oval

The team came into the season opener with a high degree of confidence, having spent a lot of money with Homestead promoter Ralph Sanchez renting the track for testing. During the CART Spring Training practice runs at the track in early February, Vasser was slightly quicker than Paul Tracy of Penske Racing, who was driving a Mercedes-Benz powered Penske PC25. So, it followed that the team would be confident going into the first weekend of PPG Cup competition. During the opening weekend, Jimmy was on pace with everyone except Tracy, who was dominant throughout the weekend. During practice on Friday and Saturday, there were no particular highs or lows for either Vasser or Zanardi, but the team was a little subdued when they failed to gain a front row starting berth which was expected, given the strong testing results they had achieved. Tracy won the pole, but Brazilian Gil de Ferran, driving a Reynard-Honda like Vasser's, only with Goodyear tires, qualified second and started the race on the outside of the first row.

However, the team still felt its Firestone tires were just as good as the Goodyears and the disappointment of not winning the pole quickly gave way to optimism about the race on Sunday.

Alex Zanardi gets a push out of the Nazareth pits from his crew. While Jimmy was struggling to a seventh place finish, Alex could only manage a thirteenth, out of the points.

Jimmy Vasser tackles the curbing on the street circuit at Surfers Paradise, Australia. The Reynard chassis holds up well under the punishment, so Jimmy was able to hit the curbs a little harder without worrying about breaking the suspension.

Zanardi, driving his first Indy Car race and his first race ever on an oval, was told to relax, not push it and just take it easy and learn. Meanwhile, Vasser's agenda was exactly the opposite, as he was going for the win and believed he had a better than even chance of staying with Tracy and de Ferran to challenge for the top spot.

The trouble for Vasser was Homestead's somewhat narrow corners, making passing difficult. That however was the least of the worries for Vasser, who saw Tracy run away with the race. Clearly, unless something unforeseen got in Tracy's way, the Canadian was going to have an easy run to the top of the podium. The race was interrupted by a light rain, but the end of the day came for Tracy when his gearbox failed after a late-race pit stop. That set the stage for a shootout between de Ferran and Vasser, a little game of cat and mouse.

After a late caution period, Jimmy made an exceptional move on de Ferran during the restart of the race. Gil de Ferran got hung up in traffic and Vasser was able to get around. CART would later change its rules on restarts, which would put the leaders of the race at the head of the pack and other cars, a lap or more down to the leaders, at the rear. Had this race been run under the new rules, there would have been no traffic for de Ferran to tussle with and Vasser would have had to make a more aggressive move to take the lead. Vasser took the lead and maintained an advantage for the final 32 laps to the end of the race, but it wasn't the kind of dominating performance every driver dreams of. Vasser would not likely have caught Tracy, had a mechanical problem not occurred. Interestingly, it was his 10th top 10 finish in the last 12 races, dating back to the 1995 season, showing that Vasser was among the most consistent drivers in the series.

Zanardi was a different story. After a pit stop, his left rear wheel came off, causing him to spin

For most of the race in Australia, Jimmy Vasser was all alone on the race track. The event is run on the city streets of Surfers Paradise, along the beaches of the Pacific Ocean.

and hit the wall. It wasn't his fault and the team assumed responsibility.

To a degree, Vasser had been feeling the pressure to notch that first victory. He had come into the series in 1992, having finished second to the late Jovy Marcelo in 1991 in the Toyota Atlantic championship. After trying to get a program running with long-time friend and mentor Jim Hayhoe, he signed with Ganassi for the 1995 season.

His Homestead victory took away any possible stigma from Portland and established Vasser as a front runner in the series. Still, Vasser was looking for the perfect, or near-perfect race weekend to notch his belt.

For Jim Hayhoe, it was an emotional moment. His young protégé, whom he had met on a boat five years prior, was now in victory circle at a PPG Cup event.

"I was speechless—literally I couldn't talk because I was so choked up," said Hayhoe.

"Getting to know Jimmy in 1995—and 1996 was only his first complete season in Indy Cars where he got to run all of the races—it was certainly a high point for him, but there would be other wins which meant more to him," Anderson noted concerning the win.

Race 2
March 17
Rio 400
Nelson Piquet International Raceway
Rio de Janeiro, Brazil
1.3-mile Oval

Alex Zanardi's misfortunes at Homestead might have dampened the spirits of a lesser driver, but at Round 2 at the Emerson Fittipaldi Speedway oval, the world of Indy Car racing got its first good look at just how talented the Italian really was.

Anderson quickly found out in testing that the longer Zanardi is at a race track, the quicker he goes, and that he's a quick study.

"He's magnificent at working with the car and engineer," Anderson said. "I don't think I've ever been with anybody who understands the race car at speed better than Zanardi."

The qualifying order played a large role in the success of the Target team in Rio, as Zanardi drew a high number, and so did Vasser. Bryan Herta was the first car out and found himself the victim of terrible track conditions. The Ganassi cars were among the last five to go out, and from the beginning of the qualifying session to the final stages, the track temperature cooled nearly 15-20 degrees. That was an advantage because the cars did not slide as much,

The short ovals were a big disappointment to the team in 1996, as neither Jimmy Vasser nor Alex Zanardi could attain any measure of success. Jimmy's crew watched the action at Nazareth and the facial expressions tell all about how Jimmy was doing.

getting far better grip than the early runners. Zanardi won the pole with a 167.084 miles per hour run.

The Vasser team had been struggling throughout practice, while engineer Morris Nunn had Zanardi's car almost perfect right out of the box. Engineer Julian Robertson and Vasser were struggling with the #12 car and actually took some of the #4 car's setup numbers in an effort to improve Vasser's speed. The cooperation between cars in Rio was an example of the kind of mutual effort Ganassi expected of his two crews. Like other Indy Car teams, Ganassi's would share everything through qualifying, then run hard against each other on race day. The strategy worked as Vasser's 166.952 miles per hour was second quickest.

Rio was new to all of the CART teams, and naturally nobody had tested there, but when the Ganassi team got to the track, they quickly discovered that this oval was not like any other they had ever raced. Four-time Indy 500 winner Rick Mears, who serves as a consultant to Marlboro Team Penske, called the track a "Roval," meaning a cross

Engineer Julian Robertson leans in to have a last minute word with Jimmy Vasser before the start of the Nazareth race. Crew chief Grant Weaver (left) listens in and gives the car a final visual inspection.

between a road course and an oval. The front straightaway is very long, as cars got over 200 miles per hour before downshifting and hard braking into turn one. On ovals, Indy Cars do not have to downshift as a rule, although drivers will go between fifth and sixth gear while at speed to gain advantage for overtaking. At Rio, that first turn had to be handled like a road course turn, as drivers downshifted from sixth to third gear. Turn four was

The PPG Indy Car World Series played to capacity houses at every venue, especially Long Beach. Promoter Chris Pook was able to shoehorn over 100,000 fans in the facility that day. The race is an enormous civic event.

also tricky because, by rights, there should have been a run-off area there, as cars routinely played with fire, coming ever so close to high speed contact. During the race, newcomer Mark Blundell found out why, when mechanical failure caused him to crash head-on into the outside retaining wall, causing him severe ankle injuries.

The Ganassi team studied track simulations from Reynard, but really had no idea what to expect, and it was a logical guess to come up with a beginning setup. Nunn rarely ever backs up once he has his car's setup close, and working with Zanardi, Nunn had everything going his way in Rio. Mo will make changes to the car, and if a change doesn't work, he'll back-up and continue from the point where he started. Some engineers make changes, then get lost in all of the numbers, but Nunn has the ability to stay on course.

With Nunn and Robertson sharing the information from their cars, and the drivers, Zanardi and Vasser working together, it is easy to understand why modern Indy Car teams prefer to work a two-car operation with full disclosure between them. The gathering of information is doubled. Given the drivers and engineers involved are quality professionals, the opportunity for four heads working as one is created. In short, if one goes fast, chances are the other will follow quickly. Owner Chip Ganassi insists on driver cooperation. He told Vasser, Zanardi and the engineers that they were in the deal together and that they would share everything. The team members were sensible enough to know that their success was predicated on the success of the other driver.

The race did not go smoothly for Zanardi, as he got out of sequence on his pit stops, possibly due to a communication problem. Rather than challenging for the win in the later stages of the race, Zanardi wound up finishing fourth. As for Vasser, like many Americans in Rio, he got sick, picking up a virus. The car was not good on race day, something he could drive quickly for a couple of laps while holding his breath, but not a car he could run hard and compete with against the other cars. On his second stop, the set of tires placed on the car was terrible. The team never really figured out why the handling problem occurred, as it might have been due to incorrect tire pressure, or perhaps the right side tires went on the left side of the car.

"We spooked him a little bit with that and it took us a while to get that sorted out and by the time it was over, we weren't anywhere near the front," said Anderson, recalling the incident.

Although Jimmy had an eighth place finish in the race, he lost the point lead by one marker to Scott Pruett, who finished third.

Joe Montana was an inspiration to the entire team, especially the drivers. He and Alex watched Jimmy during qualifying at Long Beach.

Race 3
March 31
Indy Car Australia
Surfers Paradise, Queensland, Australia
2.793-mile Temporary Street Circuit

A great race for a race fan is one featuring a variety of lead changes among many drivers, and a race where all the competitors finish the race in a tightly contested bunch. For a driver, a great race means winning from wire-to-wire, with no competition. Australia was close for Jimmy.

Most observers felt Scott Pruett would win the pole on Saturday with his 105.565 miles per hour run, but in the final minute of qualifying, Vasser took it away from him with a 105.583 miles per hour romp.

On race day, Vasser got into a rhythm, and ran flawlessly despite pit problems the team was

Surfers Paradise offers a festival-like atmosphere for the fans and a challenge for the drivers. The course is two long straightaways, interrupted on the front and back by a chicane, plus a series of twists on the north end. Jimmy liked it, he won.

Any victory is sweet, but Jimmy's win at Surfers Paradise was particularly satisfying because he was so dominant. Jimmy and car owner Chip Ganassi had a lot of fun in victory circle that day.

experiencing. He led the first 36 laps of the race before the first stop, giving the lead to Scott Pruett for 15 laps before taking over for good on Lap 42.

The team was having trouble getting the fuel cell full on the pit stops, so Vasser took on short fuel loads a couple of times and the team had to bring him back in for an additional stop. On the wrong day, that would have been a disaster. Pruett was fighting his fuel mileage harder than Vasser, and Vasser was able to run harder because of that. Cars are given enough fuel to complete the race distance, averaging 1.8 miles per gallon. While it is common for most cars to exceed that requirement, if a car is at or below the requisite fuel efficiency, the driver will have to lean out the engine, short shift, or do what-

ever else to save fuel. If a driver is getting good numbers, he can run flat out.

"I didn't know what happened on our first stop," Jimmy explained. "I started pulling away from Scott and I thought, 'Hey, I'm really hooked up.' I didn't know I was on half tanks."

Vasser got into a rhythm and drove a masterful race. For the last nine or 10 laps, Anderson said nothing to his driver on the radio. Engineer Julian Robertson wanted information passed on, but Anderson just said, "Shut up and leave him alone." Vasser was on a rail, as they say in racing when the car is perfect. He used the manhole covers on the Surfers Paradise streets as landmarks for the optimum braking points on the track and never made a mistake. He won the race going away.

There was another problem along the way, which Vasser and the team were able to overcome by not getting excited and just staying the course. Jimmy ran over a marker cone, which flew up into the cockpit of the car and became lodged between his helmet and roll bar. Vasser didn't allow the cone to bother him and it stayed there until the first pit stop, when it was easy removed. Again, there was little discussion about the matter.

The lack of chit-chat on the radio was the perfect example of the chemistry between Vasser and Anderson that developed over the 1995 and 1996 seasons. In 1995, since Bryan Herta was the team's main driver, Ganassi and Nunn, who always worked the races together before, chose to work on Bryan's car. Anderson, who didn't know the team would have Jimmy until January of 1995, took Vasser's car. Robertson and Anderson worked with Jimmy in 1995, so it followed that the team should remain together in 1996. Ganassi and Nunn then took Zanardi for the 1996 season.

"Jimmy and I have respect for each other and what we do," said Anderson. "We'd always talk about when I would talk to him on the radio, what part of the track he's be on. We'd pick a place on the race track and I'd always talk to him on that space. If he didn't understand me, it's no big deal. I told him that if I talked to him outside of that space, it meant the track was yellow."

Anderson and Vasser learned to build habits at the races. The habits would then turn into instinct and the two had built up two years worth of instinct. By making any kind of a change on race day, Vasser would have to start over with someone else.

Unlike baseball or any other major team sport, the strategy of an Indy Car race is not as complex. Before the rules changed, there was probably more strategy involved in terms of when to pit or stay out on the race track. Now there are basic rules to follow, which the Target team has to remember. The most important thing for Anderson and Vasser to know is where the leader is, and where their car is in relation to the leader.

Anderson has to keep track of the fuel numbers. At a road course for example, the team has to pay close attention to the fuel numbers. The driver will reach what is called the "window" for making a pit stop. The team has calculated the fuel numbers and has told the driver that he may pit anytime after a certain lap, but before the final lap of the window of opportunity.

For example, if Vasser wasn't in the lead, he would have had to pay close attention to the leader. Depending on where the leader is on the track, Vasser may have had to make an additional lap before coming in to keep on the same sequence as the other drivers, and to not, in an artificial way, put himself a lap down if the leader stays out on the track.

By knowing where the other cars were in relation to Vasser—Pruett in particular—Anderson was able to plan his pit strategy to keep his driver in the front of the pack. The fundamentals of the game came into play.

"I am so proud of the effort put forth by this team," said Ganassi. "As competitive as this series is, it's very difficult to score maximum points."

Jimmy took a five point lead over Pruett into Long Beach.

Race 4
April 14
Toyota Grand Prix of Long Beach
Long Beach, California
1.590-mile Temporary Street Circuit

Michael Knight is widely regarded as being one of the best, if not *the* best press agents in the business. Scoring a major coup, Michael arranged for MTV to follow Jimmy around at three races: Long Beach, Nazareth and Michigan.

The MTV Sports segment was perfect for Vasser, who "really looked like he was a part of the MTV generation," according to the MTV producers.

Vasser had the MTV Sports Crew in tow, and it must have worked because he would eventually win two of the three races MTV visited. It was a diversion from the pressures of war and Vasser seemed to enjoy it.

Chip Ganassi, Joe Montana and Jimmy Vasser had a lot to be happy for in Long Beach. It was Jimmy's third win in just four races. Vasser was now leading the standings by 23 points.

Because of the success down-under, Vasser was expected to roll out onto the streets of Long Beach and be competitive, which he was. However, Long Beach belonged to Gil de Ferran, who was completely dominating, relegating Vasser to runner-up status all day. Jimmy qualified third and stayed there for much of the day.

After getting pushed into the background for the first three races by Firestone, Goodyear came up with an exceptional compound for Long Beach, giving de Ferran a distinct advantage over the Target team. The equipment was essentially the same—Reynard/Honda—but the tires made the difference.

It was de Ferran's race. The Hall team got the setup exactly right and clearly was the class of the field. Although the Target car was good that day, it wasn't as good. However, the failure of a small mechanical part caused the end to de Ferran's day, as suddenly the bright yellow car slowed on course and Vasser darted by and claimed the victory.

"We knew we couldn't catch Gil unless he had a problem," Vasser said.

"They say sometimes you'd rather be lucky than good and today, it seems like we were lucky. The championship was obviously a goal of ours at the start of the race season, but you've got to take it one race at a time. This is a great moment for Target/Chip Ganassi Racing. The Honda engine and Firestone tires are definitely the combination of choice."

The team wasn't going to apologize for winning. In 1978, for example, Al Unser had a one-lap, plus lead on the field at the Milwaukee Mile, but within sight of the finish, ran out of fuel and coasted to a stop. Rick Mears got around to claim his first victory and later expressed his sympathy for Unser. The legendary A.J. Foyt told him, "Don't apologize, you'll lose more races like this than you'll ever win."

Zanardi had a bad day, as he made a mistake trying to get past Bobby Rahal. He tried to make a pass in an ill-advised spot and both cars wound up in the tire barrier. It was a painful learning curve for Zanardi, who was running second to de Ferran at the time of the accident. Vasser was running third, but was showing no signs of catching his Target teammate, who in turn, had nothing for de Ferran.

Vasser was consistent, and it paid off that day. More importantly, he was leading the standings by 23 points.

Race 5
April 28
Bosch Spark Plug Grand Prix
Nazareth Speedway
Nazareth, Pennsylvania
1-mile Oval

If there was any area where the Target cars were weak during the 1996 season, it was on the short ovals, those pesky one-mile circuits. The team was not able to test at Nazareth, which became an extreme disadvantage for Alex Zanardi, who did not even see the track until the team unloaded on Friday for practice. Vasser had done well at Nazareth in the past, but the team couldn't come up with a handle on any kind of consistency for the #12 car, making Vasser's weekend a long and unpleasant adventure.

"We were out to lunch when we showed up and we were out to lunch when we left," said Anderson, summing up the entire event.

The more a team struggles on a race weekend, the more behind it will eventually become. Teams spend the majority of their time testing in preparation for race weekends, and teams that do not come prepared are often destined to finish at the rear of the pack.

CART reduced the practice time on Friday by 30 minutes, as a cost-saving measure, so any teams needing that time suffered. The team was relying on notes from the previous season. But in 1996, although the chassis were similar, the team was using the Firestone tires instead of the Goodyears, making the setup of the car a completely different equation. As a result, the team learned more about the Firestones because it received more information from Firestone than it had from Goodyear in terms of spring rates and other setup numbers.

Vasser was on the front row in 1995, but during the race the car went loose and eventually he dropped out. In 1994, with Michael Andretti at the wheel, the team was not competitive. In short, the team had never been competitive on a short oval.

Vasser had a mediocre run, but came out with points. Zanardi crashed on Saturday, but had no major incident on Sunday. The day belonged to Michael Andretti, who won before his hometown fans.

Still, Jimmy was holding on to a 20-point edge over Al Unser Jr., who finished third and started to amass points that would eventually give Jimmy fits in the late season.

> "As competitive as Indy Car racing is right now, I think you have to be aggressive and go for what you believe will make your team a success. All of us on the Target team are excited about our prospects for 1996."
> Jimmy Vasser
> Driver #12

CHAPTER FIVE

90 DAYS OF MAY

Race 6
May 26
U.S. 500
Michigan International Speedway
Brooklyn, Michigan
2.0-mile Oval

Traditionally, PPG Cup teams would setup residence at the Indianapolis Motor Speedway for the month of May and prepare for two weeks of practice and two qualifying weekends for the Indianapolis 500. However, in 1996, everything changed. Target/Chip Ganassi Racing did not race in its hometown, and nearly all of the CART teams stayed away from the Indy 500.

For the first time since 1979, the world of Indy Car racing was divided in 1996, as the Indy Racing League (IRL), under United States Auto Club (USAC) sanction, was started as an alternative to the CART-sanctioned Indy Car series. Citing escalating costs, the lack of American drivers, and a perceived unlevel playing field in the sport, Tony George, president of the Indianapolis Motor

Speedway, spearheaded the formation of the IRL to create Indy Car opportunities for a wider range of participants.

The new IRL would stage three races in its first season, as 200-mile events at Walt Disney World and Phoenix International Raceway would precede the Indy 500. As an incentive for teams to run the entire IRL series, the league instituted a point-multiplier system. Simply stated, the point multiplier would give IRL teams a guaranteed entry into the Indy 500. The procedures for qualifying at Indy were also changed to reward a maximum of 25 spots to IRL regulars, given their ability to meet the necessary standards to make the 33-car starting field at the Speedway.

When the Indianapolis Motor Speedway changed the qualifying procedures for the Indianapolis 500, Chip Ganassi and the owners of Championship Auto Racing Teams decided not to enter the race. They launched their own event, the U.S. 500, which ran on Memorial Day weekend at the Michigan International Speedway, opposite

Jimmy hoists the Vanderbilt Cup high over his head after winning the U.S. 500. Chip Ganassi couldn't have been happier, flashing that familiar grin.

After winning the pole for the U.S. 500, the team swamped Jimmy Vasser with congratulations. Success is predicated on every member of the team doing his job to the highest possible standard. After Vasser's crash in the beginning of the race, the subsequent activity in the pits was a testament to the strength and depth of the teams in CART. Vasser radioed in to Anderson, and a back-up car was rolled into the pit lane immediately.

Indy. CART immediately dubbed this race "The Real 500," because most of the recognized stars of Indy Car racing, such as Al Unser Jr., Michael Andretti and Emerson Fittipaldi, were all CART drivers. The IRL could only boast of a couple of widely-known drivers, like 1990 Indy 500 winner Arie Luyendyk, Roberto Guerrero and new rookie sensation Tony Stewart. The Speedway maintained

that the Indy 500 made stars and that the stars of CART became stars because of the Indy 500. The CART people believed the stars of Indy Car racing were known because of the strong series and its international appeal.

Under the surface, Tony George asserted that he believed the IRL concept, which would lead to the establishment of a new set of rules for 1997, lowering the initial purchase cost of the Indy Car equipment, was in the long-term best interest of the sport. The CART owners, meanwhile, felt George was trying to capitalize on their hard work over the years in building the PPG Indy Car World Series into the most competitive open wheel series in the world. In short, it was a power struggle and a fight over the very definition of what Indy Car racing is.

While the political climate of the race made for some off-track fireworks between CART and the Indianapolis Motor Speedway, the on track activities gave the Target/Chip Ganassi Racing bunch an opportunity to lay claim to the top of the PPG Cup world during the month of May. The U.S. 500 would turn out to be memorable, in many different ways. But specifically, the 1996 U.S. 500 was the one time Indy Cars have raced opposite Indy Cars on race day during the Memorial Day weekend.

In early 1996, CART made the decision to run against the Speedway and compete for the hearts and minds of the race fans. A massive publicity campaign was instituted and in just four months, and a brand identity for the U.S. 500 had been firmly established. Rather than having one title sponsor, CART sold associate sponsorship packages, at $250,000 a throw, and paid for the race. In fact, CART reported that over 110,000 people were in the grandstands that day, although the qualifying weekend, held two weeks prior, suffered because of cold weather, and fan attendance was minimal.

For many of the teams, it didn't feel like the month of May. For the Ganassi operation, being headquartered in Indianapolis was almost like being behind enemy lines, as the new Indy Racing League was gaining momentum in Indianapolis. Although, the change in qualifying format which forced the CART teams to pass on the event, also prompted thousands of race fans to say no to the Indianapolis 500 in favor of the new U.S. 500.

The team wasn't concerned about not going to the Indy 500, as the U.S. 500 would serve new challenges. Teams should not have time for politics. Drivers race for their owners, so any time spent on discussing the political ramifications of the Indy 500/U.S. 500 struggle would not serve to

After the euphoria of winning the U.S. 500 came a big let down in Milwaukee, a short oval, where the team had no success at all. Tom Anderson (left) gets the bad news from Jimmy.

advance the cause of winning. During the month, however, all the CART teams were watching the Indy 500 closely. Most racers had spent their entire lives working to become winners at the Indianapolis 500—and it is still the most talked-about racing event in the sport. CART wanted its teams to forget Indy and join the cheering section for the U.S. 500, but the emotion during that event was flat. Teams still wanted to be at Indy.

For Target/Chip Ganassi Racing, its race was the U.S. 500, and all effort went into the preparation for the event. The disaster at Nazareth was behind them and the team knew the Reynard/Honda/Firestone would be a factor at Michigan. The team took advantage of several Firestone test days at MIS, although in early Spring, Michigan can be a cold place and the team froze during those sessions. The first day of running had an ambient temperature of 35 degrees.

"Why we didn't kill Vasser from frost bite I don't know," said Tom Anderson, describing the miserable weather conditions at the April tire test.

However, the team got its reward in May. Vasser and Zanardi were both strong runners. But for so many, the month of May didn't have the same excitement and special feeling, because for the first time, their big race was not at Indy.

53

For most of the season, the rest of the competition just saw the Target car as a blur of red and gold.

"May didn't feel like May," said Anderson. "There was a hollow feeling. Our shop is in Indianapolis and we were living behind enemy lines. The local paper was against us. It wasn't a lot of fun to be in Indy in May in 1996. The U.S. 500 was like an outlaw deal and something that CART decided we needed to do. Some very good sponsors stepped up and put up a hell of a lot of money to make it happen."

The Target drivers also stepped up. Jimmy won the pole with a 232.025 miles per hour run, while Alex qualified fourth, which meant he would start directly behind his teammate. Although CART tried to create a spectacle in its qualifying weekend, without a large crowd on hand, and no tradition to give everything meaning, it lacked luster.

The Sunday of Memorial Day weekend will long be remembered for the strange sequence of events before the start of the race. Many CART faithful followers believed the Indy 500 would be a disaster because of all the new Indy Car drivers, but as it turned out, the Indy 500 was a relatively clean race, and the last 100 laps proved to be competitive. Nobody could believe what happened to Jimmy as the cars were coming around for the start of the U.S. 500.

The crash before the start of the race will long be remembered. As Vasser brought the field around into turn four he made contact with middle front row starter Adrian Fernandez, which caused Vasser's car to make a sudden right turn up the banking. Vasser slammed headfirst into the wall. The debate over whether Jimmy came up and hit Fernandez, or if Fernandez veered down and hit Jimmy will likely be discussed thousands of times in the future. Jimmy would take a lot of heat for the incident, as he was the pole sitter. The actual cause and blame for the accident is a matter of opinion, but the timing of the incident was ironic. Had it been another race, at another time, it would have already been forgotten. Because the CART drivers

were so highly touted as being the "real drivers," the incident scorched through the Indy Car world. The racing world, watching in Indianapolis, looked on with fascination. The series that was to set the standard for excellence was caught in an embarrassing calamity.

But the subsequent activity in the pits was a testament to the strength and depth of the teams in CART, as back-up cars were rolled into the pit lane, almost before the last car in the accident came to a halt. All told, 12 cars were involved in the incident and all but one driver was able to rejoin the race in either a back-up car, or a repaired primary car. The delay was over an hour long, but once the race was started, the quality of the show came to the forefront, as several drivers battled at the front of the pack. Still, how Jimmy Vasser got to the starting grid for the second time may well be the real story of the race.

Vasser radioed in to Anderson to tell him he was in the wall, but that he personally was not harmed. Immediately Anderson got the troops moving to prepare the team's back-up Target car. Actually one can credit Target for making the U.S. 500 possible for the team. Oftentimes a two car team will go to the race track with three cars—one for each driver and a spare. The team had enough sponsorship money from Target to purchase the fourth car, and have a few extra crew members to maintain the fourth car for competition. Vasser had run the back-up car for a few laps on Friday to make sure it was ready. Any changes made to the primary car were made to the back-up car, so when Vasser got in his back-up after the crash, it was identical, or nearly identical to the primary car. The back-up car had a different turbocharger, but that was the only difference.

"I could see that the right side of the car was gone," Anderson explained, recalling the moments after the crash. "I saw Jimmy hop out of the car on the television monitor, so I looked down to Grant Weaver

> *"To put a back-up car out there and win is a real tribute to the Target/Chip Ganassi team. It was not as good as the first car, and we tried to make it better during the race. Every pit stop we worked on it. By the end, we had it running pretty good. It's a real credit to the team."*
> Jimmy Vasser
> Driver #12

(crew chief) and I just pointed to the other car. Grant knows the car has got to be ready, because it's insurance. We knew that it was ready, so it was only a matter telling the guys to prepare the back-up."

CART rules, unlike those of the United States Auto Club, allow for teams to field the back-up car if there has not been a complete lap run in the race. Had the crash occurred at Indy, none of the 12 cars involved would have been able to start the race unless they started their primary car. The CART rules made the Target team a million dollars that day. People will argue which rule is right, but teams have to be prepared to meet any circumstance.

CART also had a new procedure for yellow flags at the U.S. 500, which took away a lot of the immediate decision teams had to make whether or not to bring in the driver for pit stops. When the track went yellow, the pits were closed. That gave teams 20 or 30 seconds to think about pitting or staying out on the track. The Target team could now talk it over, get the driver's feedback and in general, make a team decision.

Both cars were strong in the race, but the only Honda engine failure the team had all year happened to Alex Zanardi, who was leading the race. Alex led 128 laps of the race, as Jimmy was working with the car, trying to get back into contention. The Michigan track is tough on cars and this time the bottom end of the engine failed on Zanardi's #4.

Jimmy had led the first 18 laps of the race before giving way to Alex, but during the course of the 250-lap chase, Mauricio Gugelmin, Greg Moore, Parker Johnstone and Andre Ribeiro would share the lead. Moreover, Ribeiro appeared to be in position to win, but a fuel problem forced him to slow coming out of turn four, just 10 laps from the finish.

The U.S. 500 pole carried a $100,000 Pole Award from Marlboro. Chip and Jimmy gladly accepted the money from Marlboro, but the presentation was special because Indy Car legend Rick Mears (left) was there to take part.

Vasser, by then, was dogging him and took command. Jimmy pulled away from Gugelmin and third place runner, Roberto Moreno, who was a lap down.

Jimmy won the U.S. 500 and its $1 million purse—his fourth win in the first six races. It was elation for the #12 crew and an unhappy day for the crew of the #4 car, but all wins and losses are shared by the team.

"From the team standpoint, each team shares equally in terms of the purse, so Jimmy's guys share when Alex's car wins," Anderson explained. "No matter where we finish, all the guys get the same amount in their pay check (except the drivers, who are paid on a percentage, based on where they finish). That's the easy part of it. There's the emotional drain. We had the emotional side early in the season when Jimmy's team was bringing home the bacon every weekend and Alex's team was really struggling. It was emotionally hard on Alex's team."

Vasser was in the PPG Cup lead by 36 points after the U.S. 500, and clearly he was the man to beat for the PPG Cup. It was the foremost thing on the minds of all the team members from the first race of the season.

"We never imagined going out and winning four out of the first six races," said Anderson.

"When we got past the U.S. 500 and had that fourth win, the PPG Cup was gleaming brightly in our dreams. But there were a lot of races to go and there were some people out there who could win back-to-back races, and our lead was not insurmountable."

CART deemed the U.S. 500 an unqualified success, but for 1997, CART decided to move the date of the race back to the end of July, as the traditional Marlboro 500 date was reserved for the U.S. 500. Moreover, CART stated that the goals for the U.S. 500 had been met, and the statement that needed to be made was made.

For so many drivers, winning the Indianapolis 500 is the single, biggest accomplishment of their careers, but for Jimmy Vasser and his teammates, winning the biggest race of the year, the U.S. 500, against the great teams of the PPG Cup, was more than satisfying. Still, in the minds of some of the team members, it fell short of an Indy victory, but it was close. The 1996 U.S. 500 was a one-time race, as CART scheduled a 200-miler on the Saturday before the Indy 500 for 1997. The U.S. 500 is not likely to carry the same hype, enthusiasm and importance in the future, because it is no longer the rival of the Indianapolis 500.

CHAPTER SIX

THE FAMINE

Race 7
June 2
Miller 200
The Milwaukee Mile
West Allis, Wisconsin
1.0-mile Oval

Jimmy had won four out of the first six races, but the ugly head of the short oval monster reared up again in Milwaukee. Alex was the last car to qualify before a rain shower nullified the qualifying session and brought an end to the day. That was the good news. The bad news was Zanardi hit the outside retaining wall in turn four, causing extensive damage to the car. He was not injured, but it was another start to a dismal short oval weekend. There was no qualifying because of the rain and teams lined up according to their practice times, which put Alex seventh on the grid and Jimmy well back in 14th.

The team tested at Milwaukee, but did not run well and did not improve on race weekend. Vasser held on to climb into 10th, but was not spectacular, finishing the race four laps off the pace. It marked the first time all season that he failed to crack the top eight, but he still led Unser in the points 97-75.

The new restart rule came into play, as on a late race restart, Michael Andretti, with no lapped cars in his way, was able to mount a good charge on Unser and take the lead. While the rule hurt Unser, the restart thrilled the fans and Unser graciously accepted the situation as being in the best interest of the fans. Jimmy was way down from the leaders, so when the yellow came out, he had to give way to the leaders. He could have been aggressive, but chose to allow the leaders to race.

Alex meanwhile, struggled along and finished 13th, out of the points.

Alex Zanardi most likely passed more cars in Detroit than any other driver, but had little to show for it. Under the new CART rules, drivers a lap down must fall behind the cars on the lead lap after a caution period. Alex had to go behind cars he passed several times because of the cautions.

The brightly painted PPG Pace Cars await the signal to roll away from the pits shortly after the starting command for the Marlboro 500 was given. The crews raise their hands in the air, signifying their car's engine has fired.

Race 8
June 9
ITT Automotive Detroit Grand Prix
Belle Isle Park
Detroit, Michigan
2.1-mile Temporary Street Circuit

Jimmy Vasser was off the pace going into the race weekend at Detroit. On Friday he crashed and was injured. During the crash, his helmet raised up a little and bruised the nerve under the backside of the ear. He had vertigo as a result of the crash, which is a malady of the inner ear and effected his balance. Vasser persevered all weekend, but did not qualify well and started 20th.

The Firestone tires took the pole, as Scott Pruett turned in a strong performance, but on race day, Firestone's Achilles heel turned up. In the morning, the rains came, causing all teams to change to the grooved rain tires. The Indy Cars ran their warm-up and it was discovered that the Firestones were so bad in the wet, they had to take emergency measures. Borrowing tire groovers from Michelin, the tire supplier for the North American Touring Car Series, Firestone engineers hand grooved nearly 80 sets of tires for their customers. It helped, but not enough. The Goodyear teams drove by the Firestone teams like they were tied to a post.

Zanardi's race turned out to be a study in frustration. Alex lost a lap in the wet, but began to pick up positions once he got back on the slick tires. In fact, he was really beginning to hook up, but every time the yellow came out, he was forced to get behind all of the cars on the lead lap for the restart. Once the track went green, he'd pass those same cars again, trying to make his way to the front to pass the leader and get his lap back, only to have the yellow come out again. Under the old rules, Zanardi might have had a much higher finish.

Jimmy could breathe a little easier, as Unser dropped out. He picked up two points on Little Al, but Michael Andretti won again and closed to within 27 points of Jimmy.

Race 9
June 23
Budweiser/G.I. Joe's 200
Portland International Raceway
Portland, Oregon
1.922-mile Road Course

With eyes fixated on Jimmy Vasser, the Target/Chip Ganassi Racing Team began to show its full potential, as a new star rose on the PPG Cup horizon in Portland.

Alex Zanardi carried the team colors, and in the process, began his ascent to the top of the PPG Indy Car World Series leader board. Portland suited Zanardi perfectly, and engineer Morris Nunn came to town with a good idea of what the car would need to be fast, consistent and competitive. Firestone, embarrassed in Detroit, came to Portland with a good tire.

Jimmy had his worst weekend of the season, as he did not score any PPG Cup points. He qualified in the top 10, but a single rain cloud caused all of his problems. The team could see that one rain cloud coming in during the race, and for a while the rain fell. Vasser wanted to come in for a tire change during the wet, but Anderson said no. It was the right decision, but in retrospect, Anderson felt he should have sold the decision to his driver, as Vasser was not at all in agreement. Jimmy spun off course, but prior to the spin, despite the wet, he was running two seconds per lap quicker than his teammate, who was leading the race.

Jimmy Vasser takes care of last minute details with the crew before the start of the Cleveland race.

"I think Jimmy was a little frustrated because he wanted to have a Zanardi weekend," Anderson explained. "He has a lot of family and friends up there and that was a big weekend for him that kind of fizzled out."

However, Vasser did not give up. He kept on running his race, but fell short of scoring points.

Meanwhile, Alex was becoming a star. The league was starting to take notice that Zanardi was not just another driver, but a serious contender for the title. He won the pole with a 117.209 miles per hour lap and in winning the race, Zanardi proved that Target/Chip Ganassi Racing not only could win races with both cars, but could dominate as well. Zanardi's first Indy Car win was a calling card on the rest of the teams. The way the team looked at it, either they were doing everything right, or the rest of the teams were having problems. Both drivers had won races, and just as important, Vasser was finishing all of his races, giving the team the opportunity to score points.

"Alex didn't arrive until he got to Portland, which is where the #4 car side of the team started to step up," said Anderson. "It's also when the tide turned. Things started to move away from Jimmy at that time and we went into our late-summer slump. The charisma just shifted from one wall to another in the shop."

Race 10
June 30
Medic Drug Grand Prix of Cleveland
Burke Lakefront Airport
Cleveland, Ohio
2.359-mile Temporary Circuit

Jimmy Vasser got right back on track with a 144.932 miles per hour pole position on the shores of Lake Erie. Seemingly, his teammate's dominant performance at Portland was just a one-time occurrence and the PPG Cup leader would regain his status as the man to beat.

Cleveland is a funny place. Because the track is an active airport, teams cannot come to town for a test session, and the course changes slightly from year to year. The track is wide, rough, and it's the only road course track in the series where fans can see the entire circuit from the grandstands. However, because it is flat and there are no distinguishing landmarks on the circuit, it is difficult for drivers to pinpoint their braking areas. The airport is built on a ground fill and the bumps move around.

Jimmy's qualifying time on Friday stood and he started the race from the pole. Zanardi was not far behind and on race day, the Target cars started side-by-side on the front row. The question often arises in these situations, are there any team orders?

"After the Sunday team meeting, Chip holds a private meeting with the drivers," Anderson

Alex Zanardi had a frustrating weekend at Detroit. He fell a lap down early in the race due to the rain, but was one of the fastest cars on the track in dry conditions. However, because of several caution periods, he could not make up his lap, due to the new CART restart procedures.

said. "He used to throw the rest of us out of there. He had something to say to them after we left the room. I used to ask Vasser if there was anything I need to know about, and he'd say 'nope.' Going in the Cleveland race, there were no special orders."

On the first lap of the race, Zanardi got around Vasser in the tricky turn one and took the lead. As the race wore on, it was obvious that Zanardi's car was more consistent and that Vasser had little chance of mounting a charge on his teammate. However, his problems began under caution early in the race when Anderson made a call he

After a reasonable qualifying session, Jimmy Vasser and all of the other Firestone drivers found themselves at a severe disadvantage in the rain at Detroit. The Goodyear rain tires were superior and Firestone launched a large development program immediately after the race.

would later regret. He kept Vasser out on the race track during the first caution of the race.

"Vasser is the kind of guy who has to lead, or be up front," said Anderson. "I don't think he's the type of guy who works well when he's out of sequence with the leaders and he's running 16th."

Vasser's day went from bad to worse when he collected a bright orange road cone in his front suspension while trying to pass Paul Tracy. That necessitated an unscheduled stop. Meanwhile, Zanardi was having a great race and hooked up with Gil de Ferran late in the contest. However, it all came down to the numbers and de Ferran ran longer on his final tank of fuel and that proved to be the winning difference. The Hall team ran the numbers on fuel consumption and made a good call, keeping their driver out on the race track, when others figured he would have to come in late in the race for a 'splash and go' pit stop. Zanardi ran a super race, but had to settle for second, even though he was the faster car.

After the race, there was no discussion of the decision to keep Vasser out on the track, as Anderson was so angry over his decision that he might have shocked Jimmy. Anderson told him it was his fault, not Jimmy's, and also took the blame for Jimmy picking up the cones in his front suspension. Had Vasser not been put in the position of having to challenge Tracy, Anderson figured, there would have been no cones to contend with.

Race 11
July 14
Molson Indy Toronto
Canadian National Exhibition
Toronto, Ontario, Canada
1.78-mile Temporary Street Circuit

Toronto's street course had changed slightly from the year before, as an enormous construction project forced a change in the front straightaway. In years past, the front straightaway was not so much straight, but a very high speed, sweeping left-

The Budweiser/G.I. Joe's 200 at Portland International Raceway was Alex Zanardi's weekend, as he proved to be the dominant car and too much for anyone, including Jimmy Vasser to match. That race showed that the Target/Chip Ganassi team had muscle with both cars at any race.

hander. The pits were curved as well, following the contour of the race track. The new exhibition halls across the way straightened that portion of the track and the pit area as well.

The track was not as different as the team thought it would be, and quickly Alex Zanardi took the lead, as Vasser struggled on the first day. The team had expected Jimmy to be quicker, as he was on the front row the year before. The #12 car was expected to produce big results, but again the team was off. Engineer Julian Robertson got together with Mo Nunn and tried some of Zanardi's setup on Jimmy's car, but it did little to make the point leader any faster.

Alex was king of the road, and led several laps before giving way to eventual winner Adrian Fernandez. Zanardi's race was cooked in the pits as a very long pit stop caused him to lose nearly 15 seconds to Fernandez, who took the lead eventually on a restart. All year, it was almost a given that the Target team would get their drivers out of the pits quickly, so the Toronto experience was the exception to the rule.

Even though Alex Zanardi dominated at Portland, there were still some tense moments during the race, like when the rain clouds began to gather. It's obvious Joe Montana was not just another observer, and no doubt Chip Ganassi, trying to stay calm himself, learned from Joe's ability to handle pressure.

The timing of Jimmy Vasser's first pit stop at Cleveland put him back in the field and out of sequence with his teammate and the rest of the leaders. Tom Anderson made the call and admitted freely that it was a mistake. Note the television crew dressed in blue (left). They are from Brazil.

Little attention is given to the men who perform the pit stops, but there is no doubt that the Target crews kept their drivers in the thick of the races all year by executing snappy pit stops, with very few mistakes. On Jimmy's #12 car, Grant Weaver, the crew chief, changed the outside front tire, while Jeff Carter did the inside front. Tim Keen is the fueler, Scott Horner is the vent/jack man, Gary Deal changed the inside rear and Devin Pricket did the outside rear. The group stayed healthy all year, which is important because pit stops are highly choreographed movements, requiring perfect timing and, believe it or not, athletic skill.

On the #4 car, Rob Hill, the crew chief who normally does the outside front tire, went down with a heart problem before the Toronto race. He underwent emergency heart surgery to implant a pacemaker, as he had gone into cardiac arrest as a result of Lymes Disease. His recovery was quick and complete, but the team was stunned when he went down.

The hospital staff said they had never seen a man, with so few heart beats per minute, still talking. Hill recognized one of the nurses at the hospital and talked to her as they wheeled him down the hallway.

"He was amazing, a real example of a positive attitude and how people should be when they're sick," said Tom Anderson. "We were joking with him about the battery in the pacemaker and he said all he needed to do was turn it up a couple of notches and return to work. Here's a guy in his mid-30s, strong as an ox and he goes down. It makes you appreciate being able to come to work in the morning."

The rest of the team on the #4 car included outside rear tire changer Brad Filbey, inside front man

Alex Zanardi leads the pack through turn nine at Portland before the start of the race. That's Scott Pruett on the outside.

"Every time I put on my helmet and close the visor, I'm trying to win. After the U.S. 500, we had some things happen to us that could have happened to anyone. At the mile ovals, Nazareth and Milwaukee, we couldn't stop the cars from going loose. At Detroit, I hit the wall during practice and that resulted in vertigo. I missed an important test at Mid-Ohio because of that and we weren't 100 percent at Portland, where I spun in the rain, and didn't score any points. I got the pole in Cleveland, but we got off-base on our pit-stop strategy and then I spun. We struggled with the setup in Toronto. Back in Michigan, we set a world record in qualifying—that was great to beat Mario's (Andretti) record—but had one problem after another with the car during the race. The important thing was we were finishing and adding to our points. Al (Unser) Jr. and Michael (Andretti) took runs at us but never got ahead in the points, although Al got to within one point after Michigan. The other important thing that at that stage of the season was Alex started to feel comfortable in Indy Cars and got on a roll and that took points away from some of the other drivers."
Jimmy Vasser
Driver #12

Wayne Westplate, inside rear changer Rick Davis, fuel man Wayne Gape and air/jack man Steve Gough.

The Toronto race was tragic, as a horrifying accident in the final five laps of the race claimed the lives of driver Jeff Krosnoff and course marshal Gary Avrin. Street courses are regarded as being among the safest circuits in the sport, and since 1986, the first year of the event, nothing has come close to the events of July 14, 1996. The officials of Championship Auto Racing Teams and the car manufacturers have worked tirelessly over the years to produce a set of rules that will maximize driver safety. But racing is inherently a dangerous sport and no race course, or race car, is completely safe.

Anderson and Vasser talked about the accident and agreed that each person would handle it their own way. Drivers understand that racing is dangerous, but don't truly believe that the next accident would end their career through injury, or perhaps even be fatal. Otherwise, as Parker Johnstone said in recalling the accident, the driver wouldn't get into the car and go out there. Little was said within the team about the fatalities.

Vasser had known Krosnoff since his childhood and the two were close. Unlike Jimmy, who came up through formula Ford and Toyota Atlantics, Jeff had gone to Japan to run F3000 and had come to Indy Car racing in 1996 in much the same way Alex Zanardi had, at the urging of Reynard. Krosnoff had also run the Toyota engine in Japan, so he had ties there as well, but his path to the PPG Cup was unusual for an American driver.

Racing has improved significantly over the years in terms of its safety rules and procedures. In the 1960s and prior, the sport routinely would lose several drivers a year. Formula One, CanAm, World Endurance, Indy Cars, NASCAR and other groups had to deal with fatalities regularly. However, the advances in safety make fatalities the distant exception to the rule. Even in spectacular crashes, when the car looks like it is disintegrating, the driver more often than not walks away without a scratch. It has been an evolutionary process over the years, and safety will remain the priority for any sanctioning group.

Jimmy got an eighth place finish, his best since the U.S. 500, but Unser was closing quickly. The lead was a scant eight points.

Race 12
July 28
Marlboro 500
Michigan International Speedway
Brooklyn, Michigan
2.0-mile Oval

With all of their success at the U.S. 500, people expected the Target drivers to be licking their chops at the notion of returning to Michigan for the Marl-

Jimmy Vasser enters the pits at Portland. Although the track is a permanent facility, the main straightaway is actually a drag strip. It is extremely wide and leads to the Festival Curves, a hard, right-hand, left-hand, right-hand combination.

boro 500, but there are no guarantees in racing and certainly no guarantees at MIS. Michigan is never a given, because 500 miles is always a tough race.

Indy Car racing is a precise and technical sport, and sometimes the smallest factors cause major problems for the teams.

For example, the ambient temperatures in May were much cooler than in late July. The higher temperatures in July alone were the cause for wheel bearing failure in six Reynard cars, meaning Target/Chip Ganassi Racing had a major problem to deal with on the Marlboro 500 weekend.

The team believed that the best package going into the race, for the Marlboro 500, was the Lola/Honda/Firestone combination. The Tasman Motorsports Group, and its drivers Andre Ribeiro and Adrian Fernandez would benefit from the less drag the Lola would produce. Given that the Honda engines were equal, and the Firestone tires would show no appreciable difference, the Lola would then be the key factor. As it turned out, they were right.

Still, Vasser won the pole with a track record of 234.665 miles per hour and Alex came in at 233.643 miles per hour—second quickest. Rookie Greg Moore was third fastest at 233.501 in a Mercedes-powered Reynard. Al Unser Jr. was next in his Mercedes.

Alex Zanardi is strapped in and ready to qualify for the Marlboro 500. Note the flags at half-mast in tribute to Jeff Krosnoff and Gary Avrin, who were killed in Toronto.

It was becoming obvious that the Mercedes-Benz engine was narrowing the horsepower gap. Honda had a distinct advantage earlier in the season, but the Target team didn't see that advantage as being large. When a team is trying to catch up in points, the advantage always looks larger than it really is. The team looked at its point lead and knew that if they fell out of a couple of races, the point lead would vanish.

Vasser's car went loose at Michigan, to the astonishment of the team. At one point during the race, Vasser had all he could do to stay even with some of the traditionally slow cars in the series. For example, at one point, Jimmy had to run hard to get around Hiro Matsushita, whose car rarely qual-

ified higher than 25th. Cars that he could easily dispatch in May, were giving him fits in July. Vasser's plight at the Marlboro 500 clearly illustrates that even a good driver can't carry a bad car. It may have been the most frustrating race for the #12 car side of the team, and the only time all year that Tom Anderson told Julian Robertson that he could not make an engineering change during the race. Anderson's experience told him to go a different direction, and through small changes over several stops, the car actually got driveable near the 300-mile mark. Vasser was able to get back into the hunt and score points with a ninth place finish. But Unser was right there, finishing fourth and now stood just one point behind Vasser.

Jimmy Vasser navigates the east end of the Cleveland track during Saturday practice. His qualifying time on Friday held up and he won the pole.

Zanardi wanted to lead every lap. He got the car high in turn three on Lap 128, got into the gray and as Anderson noted, "ran out of talent." As cars make laps on the track throughout the weekend, rubber is laid down on the racing surface, which improves grip. When a driver gets into the gray, it means the car has wandered off the groove and onto the part of the race track which does not offer the optimum traction. Moreover, the small pieces of rubber which come off the tires, called "marbles," are a hazard to navigation. Zanardi wound up in the last place he wanted to be, even though it was only about a foot off line, and it cost him his race. He hit hard, but was not injured.

The feast that had given Jimmy Vasser such a fat point lead in May, had turned into famine in June and July. By the time August rolls around in the PPG Cup season, only the best teams move forward, as budgets are stretched and the demands on team personnel seem to intensify. Al Jr. and Penske Racing had all been there before, but this was something new for Jimmy and Target/Chip Ganassi Racing.

Alex Zanardi got his first win at Portland, and with it began a late season charge to the top of the PPG Indy Car World Series point standings and a run at the title. Alex tied for second, but the position went to Michael Andretti, who had more wins on the season.

SURVIVAL

Race 13
August 11
Miller 200
Mid-Ohio Sports Car Course
Lexington, Ohio
2.25-mile Road Course

With Penske Racing breathing down their necks, the Target team had to have something go in the right direction. The Mid-Ohio race could not have come at a better time, as Vasser needed points desperately. But a new opponent came on the horizon, as teammate Alex Zanardi was flexing his muscles.

Awesome. The word is used to the point of being cliché, but Alex Zanardi had the field covered at Mid-Ohio and his race day performance can only be described as awesome.

The Target cars were ready for the circuit, located in rolling Ohio farmland. There had been an open test there earlier in the year, and Zanardi took part for the team. At the time, Vasser was still fighting the effects of the dizziness from his Detroit acci-

dent. The team also had a second test at Mid-Ohio after Toronto, which enabled the engineering staff to perfect its baseline setup for the Miller 200.

It was one of those weekends that teams dream about, as the drivers were superb, putting on an impressive performance that excited their teammates. Alex blistered the field with a 122.100 miles per hour run during the final qualifying session on Saturday, bumping Jimmy to second place at 121.584 miles per hour.

The pressure was beginning to mount on Jimmy, as Al Unser Jr. was only a single point behind in the standings and Vasser needed a strong points-earning performance to maintain his advantage. Vasser did everything right—just not right enough to be faster than his teammate.

After Friday's qualifying, the team met to discuss what setup to put on Vasser's car for the following day. While the exchange of information is helpful, it is not simply a matter of transferring the numbers from one car to another, as the individual driver has his own preferences and the car has to fit

Alex Zanardi gets doused with Miller beer after winning at Mid-Ohio. Doing the wet work are Jimmy Vasser and Michael Andretti.

his style of driving. The engineers have to balance the car around the driver's way of attacking the course. Jimmy's front suspension has to be a little stiffer than Zanardi's. Alex, meanwhile will drive around any problems in the car more than Vasser will, so the engineers had to take that into account before making any wholesale changes from Alex's car to Jimmy's.

"At the beginning of the weekend, in the short term, Jimmy's usually faster than Alex," said Anderson. "If everything goes Alex's way, he'll be quicker at the end of the weekend, or the first two days. If Alex's car is just right, I don't believe there is anyone right now who can touch him."

At different times earlier in the season, the team did put Alex's setup on Jimmy's car, but the benefits were minimal at best.

Mo Nunn came up with a slightly better setup for Zanardi and, as a result, Vasser had to run just a little harder, which caused him to use up his tires.

Rick Davis, who changes the inside rear tire on the #4 car, sustained serious foot injuries during a freak accident shortly before the start of the race. As the team was rolling the large toolbox into the pit area, Davis got his foot caught underneath the wheels and ripped tendons in his ankle and foot. Despite this painful injury, Davis refused to leave his post, saying, "We have a race to win here." Davis didn't want to let his teammates down. The team scheduled two pit stops, and Davis was determined to do his part for both. Because he was the inside tire changer, he didn't have to hustle around the car to change the tire, and only had to flop over the wall and go to work. As long as Zanardi hit his marks in the pit, Davis would be able to perform the tire change. In between stops, he sat on the pit wall and soaked his foot in a bucket of ice water to control the swelling.

Davis got his reward, as Zanardi drove flawlessly, leading nearly every lap of the race, with Jimmy running close behind in second. Alex led all but four laps, with Jimmy leading those. A one/two finish was huge, because Jimmy picked up 16 points on Al Unser Jr., who tangled with Parker Johnstone on the final lap and got no points for the day. That gave Jimmy a 17-point barrier going into Elkhart Lake.

The team thought about the point race every day. Jimmy was being coy with the press about the whole situation. The team, however, saw a different Jimmy Vasser. He was more tense out of the car than he had been earlier in the season, which his teammates felt was a justifiable reaction. After all, until 1996, Vasser had never won a single Indy Car race, and now found himself in the middle of one of the most hotly contested PPG Cup point battles in history. Jimmy was the one they were all shooting for, and the struggle late in the season was difficult for him.

Race 14
August 18
Texaco/Havoline 200
Road America
Elkhart Lake, Wisconsin
4.0-mile Road Course

The Zanardi magic continued at Road America, as he outran Gil de Ferran for his second straight pole position, posting a 140.771 miles per hour run. But unlike Mid-Ohio, Vasser was not as quick and qualified seventh on the grid.

The team tested at Elkhart Lake earlier in the summer and recorded the best times of any team, but they did not execute long, consistent runs with the Firestone tires. When the Target team tested there, the Firestone engineers were still concentrating on the development of rain tires, having been caught out at Detroit in June. Tom Anderson believed all of the Firestone teams suffered as a result of the diverted effort, but was confident the Firestone product was sufficient to keep the edge over Goodyear. The team tested different combinations of tires, and if one place stands out as being weak on the tire front, it would be Elkhart Lake. Both Alex and Jimmy blistered tires in the race, which they believed was related to the setup of the cars. Although Zanardi won the pole, Anderson was concerned about the consistency of the tires. There is a vast difference between going quickly for one lap and going quickly for 20 laps. Jimmy, who

Jimmy Vasser at speed at Mid-Ohio. Jimmy finished second to teammate Alex Zanardi. The second-place finish put Jimmy 17 points ahead of Al Unser Jr.

was the quickest during the test, was struggling. Julian Robertson had decided on a new setup for the car and when the team returned, Jimmy did not start where he left off at the test. That cost the team valuable time on the first day, as they had to return to their testing day setup sheet.

The race was strange for the Target team, as seemingly disastrous occurrences during the first half of the race turned out to be mild moments of misfortune.

Zanardi and Gil de Ferran collided on the first lap of the race, sending de Ferran off course and

out of the competition for the day. Alex was able to continue, but had lost several positions. The team feared the contact had bent Zanardi's suspension, but the car was not harmed and he went on to finish third.

Meanwhile, Vasser's day was brutal. A communication problem proved disastrous for Vasser. CART called for a full-course yellow flag, which immediately prompts the teams to call their drivers and bring them into the pits for a stop. When the yellow was called, there was a long hesitation after the call before CART decided that the pits would be closed.

The Target cars were on the front row at Mid-Ohio and finished one/two in the race, the most dominating performance of the year for the team.

During that hesitation, Anderson called Vasser in, just as CART closed the pits. Vasser came in behind Bobby Rahal and Bryan Herta, but was instructed to drive through the pits. To further complicate matters, the speed limit in the pits at Road America was 60 miles per hour, so as Vasser was making his drive through, the competition was out on course, running much faster, even under caution. Jimmy lost distance on the race track to the leaders and had to make another lap before coming in for his stop.

Meanwhile, Unser led, with the Newman/Haas drivers Christian Fittipaldi and Michael Andretti following, and Jimmy running out of the points. The point lead was once again in jeopardy. But the skies brightened as the race wore on, as Vasser picked off a few positions, then as if it were ordered from heaven for Vasser, Unser's Mercedes-Benz exploded on the final lap, almost within sight of the finish. Christian Fittipaldi had problems as well. Vasser wound up sixth in the final tally and instead of losing his lead, he increased his point lead over Unser to 21 points.

Michael Andretti won the race and got back into the points hunt.

Race 15
September 1
Molson Indy Vancouver
Pacific Place
Vancouver, British Columbia, Canada
1.704-mile Street Course

The Vancouver weekend turned out to be a study in frustration for both Jimmy and Alex, as neither had a good run. Zanardi, however, did capture his third consecutive pole position with a 113.576 miles per hour mark, while Vasser, similar to Elkhart Lake, was a few positions back in fifth.

Because the Vancouver circuit is a temporary, street course, built around the domed stadium and the new arena, on the site of the old

Alex Zanardi led all the way at Mid-Ohio, and Jimmy said, "I had nothing for him all day," meaning his car just wasn't as strong. Bryan Herta (background) ran third until Michael Andretti overhauled him.

World's Fair grounds in Pacific Place, there was no testing before the event. Alex saw the track for the first time on Friday, which turned out to be a long day for the team. The setups on both cars were off the pace. Only a strong engineering effort would bring them back into contention the next day.

Early in the race, while attempting to pass P.J. Jones on the outside going into a right-hand turn, Zanardi was forced to go wide and crashed into the outside retaining wall. He was livid and stalked back to the pits in search of anyone from the Gurney team to blame for the incident. Team publicist Michael Knight grabbed Zanardi from behind and literally lifted him off the ground in an attempt to hinder his progress towards the Gurney pit. Knight was able to redirect his driver back to the team's

transporter, where Zanardi spent several minutes cooling off before talking to reporters.

Jimmy shot himself in the foot with a pit lane violation for speeding, which put the car back in the serial and out of sequence with the other cars. Vasser had a good opportunity to finish as high as third, but the penalty pushed him well back in the pack, and he had to battle to salvage a seventh place finish. Bryan Herta was running in sixth late in the race, and just a little quicker than Vasser, who, feeling the frustrations of the weekend and the pressure of the championship race, lashed out at Herta for not moving out of the way. Vasser and Herta spoke a few days later and Jimmy apologized for his harsh words. Herta

RIGHT
Alex was in a class by himself at Mid-Ohio.

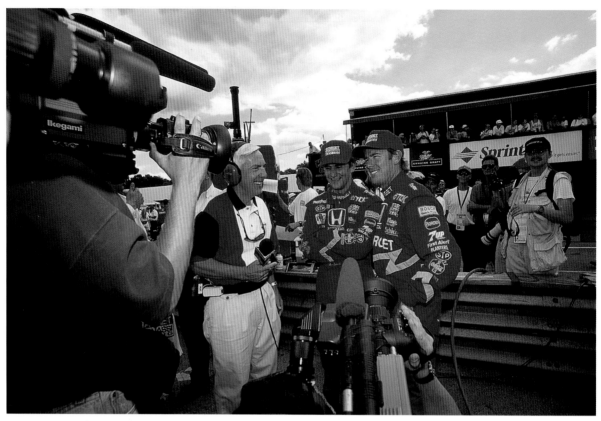

Gary Gerould of ESPN and ABC Sports, gets ready to interview Alex Zanardi and Jimmy Vasser for the Indy Car qualifying show on ESPN2 at Mid-Ohio.

> "Alex is a very good driver,
> but his real talent is in setting up his car.
> He's not afraid to try things and is willing to make
> a change right up to the last minute. I was trying
> to go to school a little on Alex and learn from
> him, although, ultimately, I have to find a setup
> that fits my style and he has to do the same for
> himself. Most importantly, Alex is a great guy, nice
> to be around, and I think we worked well together
> and that helped both of us be successful."
>
> Jimmy Vasser
> Driver #12

accepted the apology, saying that he fully understood how Jimmy must have been feeling, and that was the end of the incident.

Michael Andretti became the winningest driver of the season by capturing his fifth victory.

With one more race remaining on the schedule, Vasser was holding on to a slim 14-point lead, but his teammate Alex, because of the crash, was officially eliminated from the title chase. Now it was on to Laguna Seca Raceway, where Jimmy would have to hold off the challenges of Indy Car racing's biggest superstars, Andretti and Al Unser Jr.

RIGHT
After a terrible start at Elkhart Lake, Alex Zanardi came back to finish third in the race and got to pop a bottle of Chandon in celebration.

CHAPTER EIGHT

TRIUMPH

Race 16
September 8
Toyota Grand Prix of Monterey
Laguna Seca Raceway
Monterey, California
2.214-mile Road Course

The Championship Association of Mechanics (CAM) gave Target/Chip Ganassi Racing five year-end awards, honoring the great work of four Team Target members. Rob Hill won the 1996 Earl's Performance Products/CAM "Jim McGee" Award and the Delco Battery/CAM "Great Starts" Award. Grant Weaver was named to the 1996 Raybestos/CAM Indy Car All-Star Team. Wayne Johnson won the 1996 Penske Racing Shocks/CAM "Shock Specialist of the Year." Dick Davis was also named to the 1996 Raybestos/CAM Indy Car All-Star Team.

It is not uncommon for Michael Andretti to put together multiple wins, and Michael is used to the pressure of championship seasons, so he had nothing to lose at Laguna Seca. Andretti was 14 points behind Jimmy Vasser, while Unser was 18

back. Likewise, Unser, was not feeling the pressure, having been in a similar situation in 1995, when he was chasing Jacques Villeneuve for the title.

The mood of Jimmy's team was generally upbeat, but as Jim Hayhoe described that weekend, time was standing still. Minutes were like hours, and it seemed that the race on Sunday would never come around. The spirits were high on the #4 car side of the team, as nothing was on the line. They had been winning poles and races since Portland, and had the feeling that they were capable of winning every race. They felt Zanardi was their hero and had an aura going. The #4 side was a happy group.

The #12 car side was a little more pessimistic. The crew was starting to feel the pressure because they had finished every race of the season, but still had not put away the championship. The Portland race was the only one they failed to score points in, so in normal circumstances, a team would have already claimed the title. The feast of the beginning of the season, and subsequent famine, had

Jimmy Vasser wore his own, personalized hat.

Jimmy Vasser in action at Mid-Ohio. The Target cars finished one/two in the race.

turned into a struggle to stay ahead more than the quest for a title. They were concerned that they would be the ones that made the mistake that would cost Jimmy the championship. The press was around all weekend, asking whether or not the team was feeling the pressure. Tom Anderson had the best answer: "Not as much as the guys who are 14 points behind."

The pressure was really on Al Jr. and Michael to catch up. Jimmy was not cocky about being in the point lead, but at the same time, he was not intimidated over being chased by two world-class drivers and teams. A mature, savvy Jimmy Vasser climbed into the cockpit that weekend, did his business and qualified fifth. He was about to claim his title, but it was a different Jimmy Vasser, one more mature with a look of determination, rather than anxiety.

For Vasser, each individual PPG Cup point would be precious this weekend, so when Alex won the pole with a 118.475 miles per hour run on Saturday, his fourth in-a-row, it meant one less point that Andretti or Unser could grab. Now there was only the 20 points for victory and the one point for leading the most laps.

"This is what it's all about, being in a position to win a championship," Vasser said, trying to remain calm and give the appearance of having it all under control.

Both Al and Michael made moves to the front of the pack, but both experienced mechanical failures or problems on the track, and long before the race was over, it was obvious that Vasser only needed to bring the car home. Even if Andretti and Unser stayed out there and finished one/two,

Alex Zanardi overcame a tire blister to capture his third victory of the season with a brilliant, last-lap pass of Bryan Herta at Laguna Seca Raceway, near Monterey, Calif.

Vasser only needed a sixth or better to clinch the title. But with Zanardi out in front of everybody, except Bryan Herta, the 20 points for the lead, or the 16 points for second and the 14 points for third were being held during the race by other drivers. In short, it didn't matter where Unser and Andretti finished at that point.

Bryan Herta had the race all but in his hip pocket, and was holding off Alex on the final lap of the race when the two approached the famous "Corkscrew," a twisting, steep downhill, left/right combination, which is widely regarded as one of the most interesting turns on any circuit in the world. Zanardi had been following Herta for dozens of laps, trying to figure out exactly how a pass could be made on that part of the track. After

the first left-hander, Zanardi bolted to the inside, knowing that if Herta saw him one of two things was going to happen—there would be contact between the two, which would likely result in both cars taking each other out, or Herta would give him room and he'd make the pass. Zanardi's #4 car bounced over the curbing and into the gravel, then darted back on the track surface, with Zanardi holding on.

The move surprised the world. Even the most experienced observers of the sport were amazed that Zanardi not only got around Herta, but held on to the race car. Bryan had left Zanardi just a little too much room. Earlier in the weekend, Zanardi had gone off course right at that same spot, so by race day, he knew what would and would not work.

Alex Zanardi got a huge greeting from Joe Montana, Chip Ganassi and the team after winning his fourth straight pole position in Monterey.

"The move was very risky but well worth the risk," said Alex after the race. "As a result, I'm here smiling and he (Herta) is not smiling so much."

As calculating as Zanardi is as a driver, it's not clear whether or not he had a prayer of making that move more than once.

Herta held on for second, but Jimmy, who was running in third for a long time, lost that position to Scott Pruett, who darted by shortly after Zanardi passed Herta for the lead. Vasser was disappointed over not finishing on the podium that day, but the feelings of joy over winning the PPG Cup more than overcame any shortcomings during the race. For Jimmy, the pressure was now off. He could relax and enjoy himself.

"I know Michael (Andretti) was saying I wouldn't get much sleep, but that wasn't a problem," Jimmy recalled. "I played golf with Joe Montana the Wednesday before the race at a charity tournament I was honored to host, and it was a fun, relaxing day. That helped put me in a good frame of mind. Most of the teams had tested at Laguna before the Vancouver race and we were the quickest, so I knew the cars would be good. At least we started the race knowing what we had to do. When Alex won the pole, it meant we only had to finish sixth to win the championship, no matter what Michael did. I was cruising the first half of the race, just taking care of the car. When it looked pretty certain that Michael and Al weren't going to win, I started to push a little more. I was a little disappointed that Scott (Pruett) passed me for third at the end, but, hey, we won the PPG Cup, and that's what the main goal was all year. It was the best moment of my career.

"This was our goal at the beginning of the season," said Vasser. "We were consistent, and that's what it takes to win the season. We finished every race this season. It's a great feeling to be the PPG Cup Point champion. This is obviously the best day of my racing career. This championship is a tribute to the whole team. We owe this championship to everyone from the sponsors to the pit crew. We stuck together throughout the entire season working for this moment."

Chip had a wide smile on his face. The Laguna Seca race put the finishing touches on a remarkable season.

"I don't think there is any question that this is my best season as a race owner," said Ganassi. "To win the race the way we did is just unbelievable. What a thrill it was for this PPG Cup to come down to the last race. It says a lot about the series and a lot about our team, which I feel is the best in the business."

Time to Breathe

When Jimmy Vasser pulled his car into the winner's circle area at Laguna Seca, after finishing fourth to secure the PPG Indy car World Series title, he unbuckled his harness, stood up in the car, then jumped into the arms of his close friend Jim Hayhoe. After the years of trying to put a top flight program together, and suffering through the frustrations of having other, more well-funded teams grab the glory, Jimmy Vasser was at the top of the Indy Car world.

"There was just so much satisfaction," said Hayhoe. "All of the days, and hours, and dollars and the tremendous commitment . . . it all came out right there in a matter of a few minutes. Knowing how some people thought he was never going to make it, and how I was criticized for this and that, and we couldn't get sponsors, it was like you're vindicated. What I believed in for all these

years—and I took my first car to Indy in 1967, so I've been around it all these years—it all just happened right there."

There were moments in the season where the strain of competition and the pressure to succeed and do the best job possible for the sponsors was wearing on Jimmy—where none of the effort seemed worth it.

"Jimmy had been racing since he was six years old," said Hayhoe. "He raced go karts and quarter midgets, and it was a family activity, a lot of fun all those times. He ran really well. He had won three or four national championships in the karts before he was 14 or 15. His mom and dad were involved, his friends, Mike and Robbie Groff were there, and they had a lot of fun. Nobody got hurt. Jimmy and his dad bought a Formula Ford car, worked on it in the garage, then went up to Sears Point (California) and he put it on the pole his first time. They were having a lot of fun. Then in the Atlantics, he was running for Angelo Ferro and John Della Penna. They ran good and had fun. That's what, to him, was his whole life. Racing was fun. He was very competitive. There was not a tremendous amount of pressure and he didn't have to make all those sponsor appearances. When he was driving for me, he didn't have to make all of those sponsor appearances because we didn't have any sponsors.

"Then he goes to work for Chip and he knew things would get better. This year he starts off so hot and by mid-summer, he's 60 points ahead in the championship. All of a sudden there's pressure from everybody, not necessarily from within the team, but from outside the team. There was the crash at the U.S. 500, then the knock on the head he took at Detroit. Things start to turn around a little and he wasn't running that strong. He said to me in August or late July, he says 'You know what, Jim, this isn't fun anymore. I'm not having fun anymore' I told him that goes with the territory. Champions are made out of running good, having problems, then coming back and hanging in there. I told him if he wanted to be the champion, he had to hang in there and do all of these things. But it wasn't fun anymore."

THE CHAMP: UP CLOSE AND PERSONAL

Full name: Jimmy Vasser

Birthdate: November 20, 1965 - Canoga Park, California

Residence: Las Vegas, Nevada

Height: 5'9"

Weight: 155lb.

1995 Car: Reynard 95I Ford-Cosworth, Target/STP, No.12

Family: Parents, Jim Vasser and Roxanne Collins. Two sisters, Candice and Vicki, and a brother, Chad.

Hobbies: Golf, skiing, classic car restoration

Person I would like to meet: David Letterman

Occupation I would have pursued instead of racing: "I didn't have a back-up plan."

Personal vehicles: Chevrolet Suburban, Acura

Favorite music or artist: All types

Favorite television show(s): Seinfeld

Favorite movie: Forrest Gump

Favorite actor: Tim Robbins

Favorite actress: Emma Thompson

Favorite kind of food: Italian

My weakness: Tiramisu

Favorite thing to cook: Bruschetta

Favorite author: Tom Clancy

Publications I read regularly: Non-racing

Racing hero: Mario Andretti

Most memorable racing achievement: Podium third-place finish with Mario in 1993

Race preparation: Full night sleep; listen to loud music before race

Best advice from parents: Be honest!

What I admire in others: Honesty, integrity

Person who has been the greatest influence on me: My father (a drag racer in the 1960s and 1970s who managed my first race teams)

My philosophy on life: Work hard and you shall receive

What drives me crazy: Waiting in line; losing

Goals: Win races! Indy! Championship!

Once Jimmy won the U.S. 500, CART's big event of 1996, Vasser was a true celebrity. There were countless requests for interviews from the media and Jimmy's publicist, Michael Knight, had a full schedule of media work for Jimmy to handle, in addition to his activities on the race track. It was all new for Vasser. The pressure became so great that by Laguna Seca, Hayhoe insisted that Jimmy get some free time.

"For 45 minutes before the cars were gridded for the race at Laguna Seca, Jimmy and I just sat in the transporter and we never talked about racing," said Hayhoe. "We just visited. We both knew it could be a huge day, huge. We just sat there and didn't let it consume us."

When a team is in the position to win the PPG Indy Car World Series Championship, more often than not, a conservative tone is sounded throughout the team, as the first priority is to finish races and score points. A driver who has thrilled fans in the past with daring moves and drives his car with unbridled joy, is suddenly transformed into a more thinking and calculating driver. Racers never like second, but racers who want to finish first down the line will settle for second today.

"There is a delicate line between being conservative and taking necessary risks. There were times over the year that Jimmy and the #12 car side of the team were more conservative than we needed to be," said Anderson. "At the end of the day we won the championship by 22 points.

"We were busy celebrating at Laguna Seca, and the team dumped a cooler of water on me. It was an absolute moment of relief. We had been thinking about this since the beginning of the year. We figured it was ours to give away and we knew we would get big challenges from some of the other teams. When it happened, it was 'Thank God we've got it.'"

Alex Zanardi will return in 1997, having seen all of the tracks and knowing what to expect. Vasser, who will be starting his fourth full season in the series, has a championship under his belt and knows what it takes to win.

"I've got the best team in the business," said Chip Ganassi.

Few will argue that.

> "I hope it hasn't changed me a lot. I'm who I am. I don't have high highs or low lows. People tell me I have new obligations and responsibilities as a champion and I hope I am a good representative for the sponsors and our sport."
> PPG Cup Champion Jimmy Vasser, when asked if the championship will change him

NEXT PAGES
At speed with Jimmy Vasser on the streets of Toronto, Ontario. Jimmy finished eighth, Alex second, but the race was marred by the accident which claimed the lives of driver Jeff Krosnoff and course marshal Gary Avrin.

STATISTICS

TARGET/CHIP GANASSI RACING DRIVER'S INDEX

Jimmy Vasser #12

Miami	Rio de Janeiro	Australia	Long Beach	Nazareth	US500	Milwaukee	Detroit
Race 1	Race 2	Race 3	Race 4	Race 5	Race 6	Race 7	Race 8
S/F	S/F	S/F	S/F	S/F	S/F	S/F	S/F
3/1	2/8	1/1	3/1	3/7	1/1	14/10	20/12

Portland	Cleveland	Toronto	Michigan	Mid-Ohio	Road America	Vancouver	Laguna Seca
Race 9	Race 10	Race 11	Race 12	Race 13	Race 14	Race 15	Race 16
S/F	S/F	S/F	S/F	S/F	S/F	S/F	S/F
3/13	1/10	11/8	1/9	2/2	7/6	5/7	5/4

Alex Zanardi #4

Miami	Rio de Janeiro	Australia	Long Beach	Nazareth	US500	Milwaukee	Detroit
Race 1	Race 2	Race 3	Race 4	Race 5	Race 6	Race 7	Race 8
S/F	S/F	S/F	S/F	S/F	S/F	S/F	S/F
14/24	1/4	3/21	2/24	9/13	4/17	7/13	5/11

Portland	Cleveland	Toronto	Michigan	Mid-Ohio	Road America	Vancouver	Laguna Seca
Race 9	Race 10	Race 11	Race 12	Race 13	Race 14	Race 15	Race 16
S/F	S/F	S/F	S/F	S/F	S/F	S/F	S/F
1/1	2/2	2/2	2/21	1/1	1/3	1/26	1/1

S=Started
F=Finished

STATISTICS

Ranking by Wins

Rank	Name	Wins
1	MICHAEL ANDRETTI	5
2	JIMMY VASSER	4
3	ALEX ZANARDI	3
4	ANDRE RIBEIRO	2
5	GIL DE FERRAN	1
	ADRIAN FERNANDEZ	1

Ranking by Poles

Rank	Name	Poles
1	ALEX ZANARDI	6
2	JIMMY VASSER	4
3	PAUL TRACY	2
4	GIL DE FERRAN	1
	ANDRE RIBEIRO	1
	SCOTT PRUETT	1

Ranking by Laps Led

Rank	Name	Laps Led
1	ALEX ZANARDI	610
2	MICHAEL ANDRETTI	281
3	PAUL TRACY	214
4	GIL DE FERRAN	172
5	ANDRE RIBEIRO	166
6	JIMMY VASSER	162
7	AL UNSER JR.	125
8	CHRISTIAN FITTIPALDI	80
9	GREG MOORE	73
10	BRYAN HERTA	41
11	PARKER JOHNSTONE	35
12	ADRIAN FERNANDEZ	17
13	SCOTT PRUETT	12
14	MAURICIO GUGELMIN	12
15	ROBBY GORDON	2
16	ROBERTO MORENO	2
17	BOBBY RAHAL	1

Ranking by Laps Completed

Rank	Nam	Laps Completed
1	JIMMY VASSER	1990
2	AL UNSER JR.	1967
3	CHRISTIAN FITTIPALDI	1913
4	BRYAN HERTA	1839
5	ANDRE RIBEIRO	1759
6	GIL DE FERRAN	1741
7	GREG MOORE	1691
8	ROBBY GORDON	1669
9	MAURICIO GUGELMIN	1625
10	BOBBY RAHAL	1618
11	SCOTT PRUETT	1613
12	STEFAN JOHANSSON	1605
13	ADRIAN FERNANDEZ	1602
14	PARKER JOHNSTONE	1597
15	MICHAEL ANDRETTI	1571
16	ALEX ZANARDI	1563
17	MARK BLUNDELL	1386
18	RAUL BOESEL	1368
19	PAUL TRACY	1342
20	ROBERTO MORENO	1334
21	JUAN MANUEL FANGIO II	1299
22	EDDIE LAWSON	1282
23	HIRO MATSUSHITA	1261
24	EMERSON FITTIPALDI	1191
25	JEFF KROSNOFF	1060
26	P.J. JONES	792
27	ELISEO SALAZAR	603
28	DAVY JONES	515
29	SCOTT GOODYEAR	400
30	MICHEL JOURDAIN JR.	384
31	TEO FABI	274
32	CARLOS GUERRERO	255
33	RICHIE HEARN	233
34	JAN MAGNUSSEN	212
35	MARCO GRECO	195
36	MIKE GROFF	192
37	MAX PAPIS	129
38	DENNIS VITOLO	87
39	GARY BETTENHAUSEN	79
40	FREDRIK EKBLOM	11

Ranking by Miles Completed

Rank	Name	Miles Completed
1	**JIMMY VASSER**	**3,637.606**
2	AL UNSER JR.	3,581.396
3	CHRISTIAN FITTIPALDI	3,494.381
4	BRYAN HERTA	3,327.557
5	ANDRE RIBEIRO	3,167.517
6	GIL DE FERRAN	3,105.203
7	STEFAN JOHANSSON	3,040.480
8	GREG MOORE	3,008.895
9	ROBBY GORDON	2,995.048
10	MAURICIO GUGELMIN	2,898.054
11	SCOTT PRUETT	2,895.096
12	PARKER JOHNSTONE	2,878.186
13	BOBBY RAHAL	2,867.994
14	**ALEX ZANARDI**	**2,838.807**
15	ADRIAN FERNANDEZ	2,822.055
16	MICHAEL ANDRETTI	2,777.955
17	MARK BLUNDELL	2,574.251
18	HIRO MATSUSHITA	2,544.520
19	RAUL BOESEL	2,479.844
20	ROBERTO MORENO	2,455.578
21	JUAN MANUEL FANGIO II	2,436.455
22	PAUL TRACY	2,296.901
23	EDDIE LAWSON	2,118.777
24	EMERSON FITTIPALDI	1,879.116
25	JEFF KROSNOFF	1,724.955
26	P.J. JONES	1,428.293
27	DAVY JONES	1,066.007
28	ELISEO SALAZAR	1,036.650
29	SCOTT GOODYEAR	708.153
30	MICHEL JOURDAIN JR.	543.653
31	CARLOS GUERRERO	482.216
32	JAN MAGNUSSEN	448.821
33	RICHIE HEARN	432.010
34	MAX PAPIS	376.332
35	MARCO GRECO	341.912
36	TEO FABI	324.740
37	MIKE GROFF	192.000
38	GARY BETTENHAUSEN	158.000
39	DENNIS VITOLO	138.330
40	FREDRIK EKBLOM	22.000

PPG Indy Car World Series Championship Point System

Position	Points
1	20
2	16
3	14
4	12
5	10
6	8
7	6
8	5
9	4
10	3
11	2
12	1

1 bonus point is awarded to the driver who wins the pole.

1 bonus point is awarded to the driver who leads the most laps in the race.

There are a maximum of 22 points available for each race, or 352 for the entire 16-race PPG Indy Car World Series season.

1996 PPG INDY CAR WORLD SERIES DRIVER PERFORMANCE CHART

RANK	DRIVER	PTS	STS	RUN AT FIN	TOP FIN	TMS LED	LAPS LED	LAPS COMP *2006*	MILES COMP *3663.061 Tot.*
1	**JIMMY VASSER**	154	16	16	1	12	162	1990	3637.606
2	MICHAEL ANDRETTI	132	16	10	1	10	281	1571	2777.955
3	**ALEX ZANARDI**	132	16	10	1	26	610	1563	2838.807
4	AL UNSER JR.	125	16	13	2	5	125	1967	3581.396
5	CHRISTIAN FITTIPALDI	110	16	13	2	3	80	1913	3494.381
6	GIL DE FERRAN	104	16	11	1	6	172	1741	3105.203
7	BOBBY RAHAL	102	16	12	2	1	1	1618	2867.994
8	BRYAN HERTA	86	16	13	2	2	41	1839	3327.557
9	GREG MOORE	84	16	9	2	8	73	1691	3008.895
10	SCOTT PRUETT	82	16	11	2	4	12	1613	2895.096
11	ANDRE RIBEIRO	76	16	9	1	6	166	1759	3167.517
12	ADRIAN FERNANDEZ	71	15	13	1	2	17	1602	2822.055
13	PAUL TRACY	60	14	8	3	5	214	1342	2296.901
14	MAURICIO GUGELMIN	53	16	10	2	3	12	1625	2898.054
15	STEFAN JOHANSSON	43	16	8	4	0	0	1605	3040.480
16	MARK BLUNDELL	41	13	9	5	0	0	1386	2574.251
17	PARKER JOHNSTONE	33	15	7	2	2	35	1597	2878.186
18	ROBBY GORDON	29	16	9	3	1	2	1669	2995.048
19	EMERSON FITTIPALDI	29	12	5	4	0	0	1191	1879.116
20	EDDIE LAWSON	26	11	9	6	0	0	1282	2118.777
21	ROBERTO MORENO	25	15	7	3	1	2	1334	2455.578
22	RAUL BOESEL	17	16	5	7	0	0	1368	2479.844
23	JUAN MANUEL FANGIO II	5	16	7	8	0	0	1299	2436.455
24	JAN MAGNUSSEN	5	4	2	8	0	0	212	448.821
25	SCOTT GOODYEAR	5	4	4	9	0	0	400	708.153
26	P.J. JONES	4	10	5	9	0	0	792	1428.293
27	MAX PAPIS	4	3	1	9	0	0	129	376.332
28	HIRO MATSUSHITA	3	16	7	10	0	0	1261	2544.520
29	RICHIE HEARN	3	3	2	10	0	0	233	432.010
30	ELISEO SALAZAR	2	4	4	11	0	0	603	1036.650
31	DAVY JONES	1	5	4	12	0	0	515	1066.007
32	MARCO GRECO	1	2	1	12	0	0	195	341.912
33	CARLOS GUERRERO	0	3	1	14	0	0	255	482.216
34	MIKE GROFF	0	1	1	14	0	0	192	192.000
35	JEFF KROSNOFF	0	11	4	15	0	0	1060	1724.955
36	TEO FABI	0	2	1	16	0	0	274	324.740
37	MICHEL JOURDAIN JR.	0	5	1	16	0	0	384	543.653
38	DENNIS VITOLO	0	1	0	17	0	0	87	138.330
39	GARY BETTENHAUSEN	0	1	0	21	0	0	79	158.000
40	FREDRIK EKBLOM	0	1	0	25	0	0	11	22.000

INDEX

Anderson, Tom 12, 17, 33, 35, 44, 45, 47, 49, 53, 54, 56, 57, 61-63, 65, 69, 72, 77, 84, 88
Andretti, Michael 13, 14, 16, 49, 52, 59, 61, 77, 80, 83-86
Avrin, Gary 67

Blundell, Mark 43

Championship Association of Mechanics (CAM) 83
CART 51-54, 56, 57, 75, 77
Carter, Jeff 65
Cheever, Eddie 12

Davis, Rick 67, 74, 83
de Ferran, Gil 37, 38, 48, 49, 63, 74, 75
Deal, Gary 65

Fernandez, Adrian 54, 64, 68
Filbey, Brad 65
Firestone 33, 34, 37, 48, 49, 60, 74
Fittipaldi, Christian 77
Fittipaldi, Emerson 11, 16, 24, 40, 52,
Ford Cosworth XD 31
Foyt, A.J. 10, 14

Galles, Rick 16
Ganassi, Chip 9-11, 13, 17, 21, 24, 25, 31, 33, 40, 44, 51, 63, 87, 88
Gape, Wayne 67
George, Tony 51-53
Goodyear 33, 34, 37, 48, 49, 60, 74
Goodyear, Scott 34
Gordon, Robby 12
Gough, Steve 67
Guerrero, Roberto 52
Gugelmin, Mauricio 14, 56, 57

Haas, Carl 12
Hall, Jim 12
Hayhoe, Jim 16, 17, 19-21, 31, 33, 40, 83, 87, 88
Herta, Bryan 14, 19, 21, 47, 77, 78, 85, 86
Hill Rob 16, 35, 65, 83
Horner, Scott 65
Hull, Mike 15, 35

Indy Racing League (IRL) 51, 52
International Motor Sports Association (IMSA) 10

Johnson, Wayne 83
Johnstone, Parker 33, 34, 56, 68, 74
Jones, P.J. 78

Keen, Jim 65
Knight, Michael 47, 78, 88
Krosnoff, Jeff 21,67, 68

Luyendyk, Arie 12, 13, 52

Marcelo, Jovy 40
Matsushita, Hiro 69
Mears, Rick 41, 49
Mercedes-Benz 31, 69
Moreno, Roberto 57
Moore, Greg 56, 68
Montana, Joe 14, 15, 86

Newman/Haas 14
Nunn, Morris 16, 25, 41, 43, 44, 47, 61, 74

Patrick Racing 10, 11
Pruett, Scott 33, 44, 45, 47, 60, 86, 87

Rahal, Bobby 49, 77
Rahal/Hogan 31
Ribeiro, Andre 56, 68
Robertson, Julian 16, 35, 41, 44, 45, 47, 64, 69, 75

Stewart, Tony 52

Tracy, Paul 37, 38, 63

United States Auto Club (USAC) 51
Unser Jr., Al 10, 49, 52, 59, 68-71, 74, 77, 80, 84-86

Vasser, Jimmy 15-17, 19-21, 25, 27, 31, 34, 35, 37, 38, 40, 41, 44-49, 53, 56, 57, 59-63, 68-72, 75-78, 80, 83, 84, 86-88
Villeneuve, Jacques 83

Weaver, Grant 16, 35, 65, 83
Westplate, Wayne 67

Zanardi, Alex 15, 16, 21, 24-26, 35, 37, 38, 40, 41, 43, 44, 47, 49, 53, 54, 56, 57, 59-64, 68, 70-72, 75, 77, 78, 80, 83-86, 88